D0852740

Books by Barbara Nash-Price

Life Awareness Calendar
The Life Awareness Calendar for Kids

The Life Awareness Manual
Revised Edition

The
Life Awareness
Manual

Revised Edition

A SIMPLE RECIPE FOR LIVING LIFE

Barbara Nash-Price

CROWN PUBLISHERS
New York

Earlier editions of this work were published by
Life Awareness International.

Published by Crown Publishers, New York, New York.
Member of the Crown Publishing Group.

Random House, Inc. New York, Toronto, London, Sydney, Auckland
www.randomhouse.com

CROWN is a trademark and the Crown colophon is a registered
trademark of Random House, Inc.

Library of Congress Cataloging-in-Publication Data is available.

ISBN 0-8129-3270-6

10   9   8   7   6   5   4   3   2   1

First Crown Publishers Edition

To my children:

You are the light in my life! This book is written to help you as you grow. This book is written for you to see there can always be a better life, a life directed inward and upward and with light. Above all, it is important to find yourself, and in finding yourself you reach beyond the lower self . . .

to the higher self . . .

the real you . . .

and you can truly realize a new Life Awareness.

Mom

How to Use This Book

Dear Reader,

I wrote this book for you to pick up or put down.

Open it to *any* page and start reading. Wherever you begin is where you will find the information that you will want to hear at that moment. There is no right or wrong way to use this book. Turn to *any* section and begin to read. Try to *learn and memorize concepts.*

As I went through painful growing stages of my life, I hoped to find a book that could help me deal with "all" of it. Bookstores and libraries are packed with books on self-help topics. However, I believe in keeping it simple.

This is a small book with a powerful recipe for starting over.

All the counseling sessions, books, tapes, and seminars had little impact on me until I was ready to *search within and learn about myself.*

Happy reading,
Barbara

P.S. The Relationship Test begins on page 44. It helps tell if two people are growing together with the same value system. It reveals inner truths, telling what is important to you both.

Contents

Recipe for True Balance in Life

Most people look at life in this order:

Physical—intellectual—emotional—spiritual.

This is wrong.

To have balance in life we need to

rearrange the order of our life.

It needs to be:

spiritual—emotional—intellectual—physical.

The spirit feeds the emotion, which

balances the intellect, which directs the

physical body to perform one hundred percent.

The Life Awareness Manual
Revised Edition

My Story . . .

Sometimes something so horrible can happen, no amount of time can erase that moment. You remember it like yesterday. . . .

It was 1979. I was thirty-two years old at that time. Sitting at my desk, I had just finished reading the "thought for today" on my wall calendar. "Oh, normal day, let me be aware of what a treasure you are."

As I read this, I had been feeling very empty. This was rather ironic, since my past had been so painful and now my life was somewhat peaceful. I was married and selling real estate. With a beautiful home, a darling son, and a good husband, I should have been very happy.

I had survived the horrors of my childhood and had longed all my life for the security and stability I now had. Yet I sat at my desk thinking, Is that all there is? Strangely enough, within a few short days, an event would take place that would give me my answer in a very powerful, frightening way.

It was a peaceful, sunny morning in July. Early in the morning, with no one to help save her, my mother had been brutally stabbed to death by a drug addict of fifteen years, my very own brother. It was a defining moment in my life. The horror of my mother's murder, the anguish of knowing she died at my brother's hands, the pain of the trial and its outcome. Many would consider what I lived through to be a breaking point. I admit I wanted to just plain die. However, over the years, a fight erupted inside me. This fight kept me searching for help, perpetuating a hunger and thirst for a different kind of knowledge, knowledge that eventually was to save me from myself. But before this was to happen, there would be a period of time when I was afraid to move one step forward.

As I look back today, there was little in my marriage that actually held my interest or satisfied me, although my days were packed with much activity.

Now, years later, I have learned so many lessons. My life has little to do with my "old world" and much to do with my "inner world." A world inside me filled with love, and above all, peace. I would have given my last dollar to experience this feeling back then. Yet, when I found it, I spent not one penny.

Coming from a childhood riddled with pain and sadness, as an adult I thought my sad times were over. I had been making good choices for myself. My belief system encompassed "who I was" and I seemed fairly content with this. I fed my mind and body each day with food and pleasure. I did not see beyond this. There were a few times I would attend church. As I look back, I think I did this more out of childhood habit than a feeling of its being the right thing to do. Rather than look for an ongoing spiritual relationship, I turned to God as a 911 or an SOS, only if things got rough.

Way down underneath, I had to admit, I was still filled with fear from my childhood and recent mistakes and letdowns. Yet I chose to deal with life utilizing only the tools my family had given to me; I relied on others to guide and counsel me. I took great pride in talking at length to my friends about their problems, thereby obtaining the opportunity to disguise my own. I found an immediate release from fear in my nightly rendezvous with alcohol. To stay ahead of my problems, I filled my plate with work, events, social engagements, trips, and shopping excursions, all of which packed my day. There was no quiet time in my life, nor did I want any.

My home was a showplace, yet seldom did I spend time there. My son and daughter, at far too young an age, were shuffled off to day care and "school," as I called it. One baby-sitter after another took the place of mom. I did anything and everything to avoid coming face to face with the "real" me. I didn't know I didn't like myself, didn't know there was another life to live. I knew nothing about tuning out the outside world and tuning in to my own inner guidance. I was in control, or so I thought. So totally on top of things, yet completely unaware spiritually. I thought being a real estate agent was my one and only profession for a lifetime. How very wrong I was. I knew nothing about who I was and who I would become.

My whole world changed the day I came face to face with the unexpected tragedy of my mother's murder. Unbelievable how, in a matter of minutes, an entire life can come unraveled. Because of what I experienced, my family, my home, my job, my friends—everything around me—changed immediately, never to be the same again. I was forced to go through a period of horrifying sadness and grief. Although we are given daily choices, we are unprepared to deal with the unexpected. This is a part of life that is completely out of our control. The only way to protect ourselves from going under is to have the right tools to deal with this. I did not have the right tools. . . . It would take me another seven years after this tragedy before I would find my answers. I would continue to live in total darkness until I was introduced to a woman who brought me face-to-face with my own guardian angel, but this will be explained in more detail later on.

At this point, however, my life would change permanently.

Before this was to happen, those seven years brought me many more painful lessons. I was numb to the world around me, and my lessons gave me one opportunity after another to look for courage I did not even know I possessed.

Little by little, my lessons stripped me of all the things I held dear, everything I had built my life on. Suddenly "who I was" came tumbling down around me.

I stood there, naked in a world I had carefully constructed for myself. Stripped of my protective devices, I had nothing to save me anymore.

Afraid to live and afraid to die, I was forced to look inward. I searched for anything that could save me from destroying myself. I had to reach out in total darkness, believing there was something out there. I had to make myself go farther than I had ever allowed my thoughts to go before.

How could I have been so right? I asked myself. I can't handle what is happening to me now! Was this my just reward for trying all my life to do things my way?

My pride and my ego stood blatantly in front of all my thoughts. When you are alone, completely alone, with no support system to lean on, you begin to rip apart what you believe. You question how it put you in this place to begin with. I thought back to old habits, old ways that had been passed down to me. Ideas I had discarded and other avenues of thought I had carefully constructed around the attitudes that now shaped my life. Nothing fit anymore. I had no proof there was any one way to live life that would necessarily work.

Someone once told me that religion is not necessarily spirituality. I never knew what this meant at the time. I do now.

I had no tangible proof for God or against him; I only knew he was not there for me and I was dying inside. If there was a God out there, why couldn't he help me now? My anxiety attacks were becoming more and more frequent. The memories of the horror I had been through continued to plague me. I was no longer able to fix things for myself. Nothing was working right for me any longer.

I remembered the year before my father died. I had come home for Christmas, as I then lived and worked in Arizona. I remember the first day I saw my father after being away for nine months. All my life he had impressed me as being a big man. His build and frame coupled with his strong, imposing manner made him seem almost invincible. Now as I looked over at him as we sat together on the couch, I saw a man turned inside out. He was hollowed out. His cheeks were sunken, his color drained. A gold wedding band was taped to keep the ring from falling off the skin of his bony third finger. His eyes were sullen; they had no sparkle. Looking up, he cocked his head. "Remember, princess, the one secret weapon that destroys a man every time. . . . It's the will. If he's lost his will to live, a man's no good to anyone anymore."

Had this happened to me now? Was there no one out there to hear me?

THE SEARCH FOR MEANING

Years after the murder of my mother, I finally began to work night and day, trying to fix myself. Nothing I found could completely heal me. Scouring bookshelf after bookshelf, I bought books and inspirational tapes, but nothing worked. I visited counselor after counselor, yet fear continued to gnaw and grow inside of me like an untreated malignancy. There was a numbing sensation toward life around me, and no one could help me find what I was looking for. The emptiness was draining me, the continual fear consuming me. I could not live like this one minute longer.

Surprisingly, finding my answers was not an involved process. It was far simpler than I had ever guessed. If anything, it took time and a great willingness on my part to believe that truth is not necessarily what I had programmed it to be. I put my hands together and prayed. Suddenly, an invisible beautiful voice softly spoke, telling me I had nothing to fear, help was now with me.

It started with just one message, an angelic message, a message of hope. At this moment, I became unafraid and filled with courage. This was all I needed. I began to explore new books and avenues of thought that I had never considered. The more I read and the more I focused on quiet and peaceful tranquillity, the more obvious the answers became. Once I started trusting in my own internal guidance, I became obsessed with finding the answer to my own personal pain. I promised myself that if and when I found it, I would write it down and share it with anyone who would listen.

Something else miraculous happened too. Once I found my own higher awareness, I never had another anxiety attack again.

Life has schooled me greatly. I believe we ask for the bodies we receive, the families we were born into, and the lessons we are given to learn from. I grew so much stronger internally by giving up the belief that I alone was completely in control of my life. Gave up the idea that my past was who I was, gave up the idea that everyone else was to blame for what happened to me.

I began to feel safer by accepting the fact that I brought no good into my life by hanging on to old anger and resentments. Gave up insisting on holding the reins of control on my life exclusively. There were lessons to learn that were given to me and to me alone. My own lessons happened to be in the form of many tragic events and intense personal pain that needed to be learned and endured. God willing, I would overcome and heal from all this. Once I accepted this fact, I would grow from these lessons. My life took on a very powerful new light. When I forgave myself and others around me for actions done in moments of anger and "lower self" behavior, the guilt I had been carrying for years lifted. Reading this, you might think I had so much to deal with. Remember this: We all have our share. Each of us is given pain and tribulation to learn from. Because of the pain you endure and accept, you become a better human being.

We are never given more than the universe knows we can handle.

"Nothing will ever harm me if I don't allow it to." Tell yourself this.

I remember a time when I was particularly down and someone suggested I attend an inspirational seminar. I thought to myself, "Been there—done that."

I was busy. What new information could this hold for me? Yet I had a free ticket to go. When I got there, I remember sitting down next to an older man. He seemed too happy for my purposes. I thought, "What am I doing sitting next to him?" I'd stay until the break time, and at the first opportunity, I would leave. I had far too much real estate work to do, and I'd had enough.

Funny . . . at the break, I was sandwiched in between a few hundred people trying to make their way to and from the lobby area. There is an old saying: "When a student is ready, the teacher appears. Angels come in many disguises." I do believe this. A man reached out and touched my shoulder. I turned around. It was the gentleman who had been sitting next to me in the auditorium. "Hello again," he said. He knew nothing about me, and I knew nothing about him, not even his name. He said, "I hope you're enjoying yourself as much as I am."

To this day that man has had more impact on my life than all the books, tapes, seminars, and counseling sessions I have ever attended. Could he have been my angel at that moment?

He looked so peaceful, so content, so happy. He went on to tell me, "I lost my wife and four daughters in a house fire, but you know, I am so thankful for the lessons I have learned. They gave up their lives to teach me these lessons. I would never want to be the person I was before this happened to me." He smiled, patted me on the shoulder, winked, and just walked away. I stood there for a long moment, chills going up and down my spine. I now saw the glass was no longer half empty in my life; it could be half full. Life was what I made it, how I envisioned the promise of each day. With each event in my life, I had the ability to change. Yes, lessons would continue for as long as I was alive. Was I now willing to go on and grow positively from these lessons?

Unfortunately, it is the painful lessons we remember the most. It is the painful ones from which we learn the most. I also believe that through pain comes the fastest growth, because we grow internally. Inside—where it hurts the most. Inside, where we tell ourselves we will never, ever forget or forgive.

Throughout my life, my relationships held me back. I kept

score and I stayed angry. I was filled with blame. I sought out relationships based on where I was in my own life, and believe me, I got back relationships that mirrored who I was. The more problems I had, the more I got people with problems. While I remained stuck, I found others who were also in a rut.

It seemed uneasily comfortable.

Old, familiar patterns of relaxing were passed down to me by family. Feel uptight? Take a drink. Got a problem? Take another drink. Want to celebrate? Take a drink. These rules for living life were passed down to me. Because my family lived their lives according to this format, these were the only rules I knew.

I now needed new rules.

For many years I watched and could do nothing as my parents fought their battle of life around me. As far back as I remember, there was always sadness in my home. My parents had their own problems to deal with, always alcohol to contend with. My father and mother lived to prey on each other, seldom realizing the needs of the small children living within their care. Before my mother met my father, he left a multimillion-dollar sales position in favor of the "bottle," two years before I was born. Our family knew only poverty.

My mother's family owned a restaurant-nightclub, considered a hotspot in town. Throughout my mother's whole life, her father and mother, brothers and sisters were daily workaholics. My mother, second to the youngest and very beautiful, lived in her own world. She came from a family that emotionally brutalized her, and in return, she paid them back. She ran away from home to marry my father, give birth to her daughter, and finally leave her family, fleeing from a life of so-called privilege to live a life of poverty.

Her new life began with two large setbacks. One, she was to deliver a baby girl just seventeen days after she married. Two, neither she nor my father ever really loved each other, yet they mirrored each other well.

How do I know they never loved each other? They told each other this for the entire twenty-three years they were married. I was the baby girl my mother delivered. I don't remember my parents ever laughing, having fun, or planning any event together. Family outings and holidays were for other people. Plans and dreams sank behind dark daily dramas.

My father was self-confident, smart, tall, good-looking, with black, wavy hair, perfect nails, and deep brown eyes. I had loved everything about him in those early years. I want to say he was my idol, but I have to say he broke my heart. He had wit and genius and the gift for gab. He could run circles around anyone. Yet he took all of his talents, his good health, and his own family and threw them into the garbage.

To this day, if he were alive I would still fear one thing and one thing alone . . . the not knowing. Not knowing what he would do minute to minute, not knowing if he was drunk or sober, not knowing if he'd hurt my mother or leave her alone, not knowing how each day would turn out . . . day after day, year after year . . . melting away my childhood and my teenage years.

My father traded in his health, traded in his family, traded in his future, all for the almighty drink. No amount of money could have saved him from himself. He'd thrown in the towel, lost his will to live before I was even born.

As little children growing up, both my brothers and I had become victims of my parents' relentless need to punish each other. We were manipulated, blamed, and emotionally beaten until we were well aware of whose rules we needed to adhere to. Our own lives and needs stayed in the background.

Perhaps my middle brother, Bruce, took on the most abuse, for he was the weakest. My little brother stayed in the background. If all the tears could be taken back, I think today my brother Bruce could have survived. For he cried so much as a little boy; seldom did I hear the sound of his laughter. The belligerent attacks by my father on my brother came quickly, cruelly, and out of the blue. So often, for no apparent reason, my father would pick on my brother until tears would flow. I know now his quiet, sweet, sensitive nature just didn't stand a chance. Tremendous amounts of pain were inflicted in those early years.

Bruce learned very quickly that his father didn't like him. One never knows why parents decide not to like one of their children, only that the damage caused is everlasting.

In many ways, my brother was sheltered from the beginning by my mother. She knew there was something wrong, and in her own way, she wanted to protect him. Huge amounts of guilt were stored up inside of her. In order to deal with these feelings, she chose to overextend herself to her son. Early on, she decided she would take him under her wing. No matter how old he was, no matter what the cost to his own manhood, my mother would be his shield. Children learn quickly how to manipulate a situation: how to lie, how to cheat, how to steal. My brother would become a master manipulator. He had the best of teachers: his very own father.

At first Bruce's spirit became damaged, then it was destroyed. When my brother was in seventh grade, I remember, he brought home a science project. He was so proud of this paper; he had worked hard on it and received a grade of B+. Yet when he brought the paper into the house one afternoon to show my father, the timing was not the best. My father had been drinking all day long.

Grabbing the paper from my brother's hand, he glared at it. "If you can't get a f——— A on your schoolwork, don't bring any more papers home, understand?" He crumpled it up and threw it across the room.

My brother stared at him, then put his head down, picked up the paper, and walked away. Slowly he descended the stairs into the cold cellar. I followed him and shuddered as I watched him holding his paper crumpled into a ball. Taking a lighter from his pocket, he set it on fire. The paper went up in flames. All his work and effort now turning to gray ashes falling gently to the floor. My brother's eyes filled with tears.

In the early years, he was all you could ask for in a little boy. Bruce was slender and blond with wonderful pale blue eyes. His kind, gentle nature made him funny when you least expected him to be. His entire being cried out for approval. He so wanted to be loved. He so wanted attention. He so wanted to have fun. Heavy weights and constraints were placed on his small being at so young an age. He never had a chance to find his own personal power. I believe he came into this world with a severe handicap—he loved his mother and father and family too much. He hurt too much. He was rejected too many times. The hurt turned to anger and the anger turned to revenge. I so wanted to help him. I quietly watched as he slowly and deliberately destroyed himself. I could do nothing to save him.

My mother assumed the role of taking care of my father. She fulfilled her role perfectly. Day in and day out, she baby-sat my father and saw to his addictive needs, silently closing her eyes to what went on around her.

In so doing, she shut out her children. My father held various odd jobs sporadically throughout the year; each one ended at the bottom of a bottle. At home, my mother cursed the almighty drink. Yet when the day was over and all was said and done, she relied more and more on this temporary, sick euphoria herself. My father had his own routine, a case of beer and a pint of whiskey a day. On days when the household couldn't afford it, or when milk was purchased in its stead, my father could be known to resort to drinking alcohol-based baking extracts from the kitchen cupboards. Other times, noticeable bare spots would appear on the walls. It was understood that antiques and other valuables had been sold to purchase a "brown paper bag with the bottle inside."

Seldom was there an opportunity to have a conversation with either parent. To find them in a sane, sober, clear frame of mind to talk was rare. Often my brothers and I would lie awake at night discussing times we could trust our father to talk soberly to us. Should we stay up late into the night? Should we wake up earlier in the morning? Was there ever a time when he could be just normal? If so, we never were given the chance to see this.

We also were never given the chance to do things with our dad and our mom that would build happy memories for a lifetime. There was never any encouragement, support, and praise, so critical to building a reservoir of strength, stability, and security for dealing with life's lessons one day at a time. We were on our own emotionally at such a young age that in many ways we never knew when childhood ended and adulthood began.

By the age of twelve, both Bruce and I had tried smoking. We had often sampled the taste of beer and liquor. Although I never actually liked the taste, I found the power it held to change someone's behavior both disgusting and fascinating.

I built up substantial amounts of anger. Yet I found a source deep within me to deal with this. I had somehow figured out where to find an internal escape at a very young age. I knew where to go "inside my mind" to bury the worst of my fears deep within myself, vowing someday to relinquish them. I so wanted to show my brother Bruce how to do this, but he was far too tenderhearted. The majority of his fears and sadness came out in his tears. He tried so hard to be strong and tough as my father always demanded him to be. Yet nature plays cruel roulette. In our family my brother should have been given the inner strength that I possessed. I could handle so much more. He was too timid, too fragile. He wore his emotions on his sleeve. This was a huge mistake around my father.

Whenever you read about a tragedy, someone always remarks, "They should have seen it coming." Yes, I saw the signs that something very wrong was happening inside my home. However, the timing was never right to step in. In the early years, I was too young, too frightened, too bullied to do anything about it. As the years went by, it was sort of like walking into a home where someone smokes; at first the smell affects you terribly . . . then eventually you get used to it. It doesn't bother you as much anymore.

I realize now that as years went by, living as a child in a home with severe alcoholism and abuse problems was a lot like being in a town with a war going on. You don't know there is any other way to live. So much brutality takes place that after a while shell shock sets in, perhaps permanently. You accept emotional and physical abuse as being okay in your own life. As a child, you don't even begin to realize that's what it is.

The years after high school were somewhat of a fog. In my

early twenties, I'd decided to leave for a while and visit my aunts, move out west. This is when I remember hearing my brother was taking more drugs and losing control. This is when I lost touch with my mother's nightmare with my father. This is when my father died of cancer at the ripe old age of fifty-two, after I'd been away from home for almost a year.

When I finally moved back home, it was too late to help anyone around me. It was my time now. Time to settle down, marry, and raise my own family.

Not until years later would I understand how much my own decisions were based on my upbringing. I was brought to the awareness of why I chose to drink, why I chose relationships that were not fulfilling, why I lived a life that was filled with chaos every day and not contentment.

There was so much dark drama as a child. I actually sought it out as an adult. A peaceful life with a "healthy" partner seemed boring to my subconscious. I actually looked for partners who were indifferent, evasive—for I was going to fix them. Work that was an insurmountable challenge to some, such as selling real estate, was a breeze to me. Making a living by commission only? Why, I found this risk to be exciting, scary, and fun all rolled into one.

Living on the edge was what I was most familiar with. I had done this all my life. Problems arose when, every once in a while, I would come in contact with my "higher self" or the real me. I ached for love and affection and romance.

When I look back on Bruce and my childhood, I realize that I always knew there was a fine line drawn in the sand that divided us. This line kept my brother from knowing and wanting a better life for himself, but it didn't stop me from choosing a better life and deliberately going after this life for myself. The line lay smack on two opposing words: Fear and Acceptance. I felt the fear and did what I needed to anyway. I accepted what was going on around me and tried to get out from under it, any way and as best I could. My brother felt his fear, let it control him, and then completely gave in to it. He became a full-fledged drug addict.

On that hot summer day in July, Bruce's fear got the best of him. He had lost sight of anything meaningful in his own life. For it was too late for him to turn back now. He did something so horrifying, his own life and everyone else's life around him would immediately change forevermore.

As I look back, I recall thinking around that time, I wonder where he is? I wonder why we haven't seen him for a while? "It's good he's not around," I thought, "he only comes around for money for drugs now." Part of me was relieved, and another part of me got that familiar sick feeling whenever he came near me. There was that scared part now, that part my father had been re-sponsible for years back. Deep inside of me, the not-knowing part . . . Not knowing when my brother would pop back into town. Never knowing when he would just appear at my mother's house, not knowing what would set him off because there had been so many violent outbursts because of the drugs he had started taking in his teenage years. Constantly, his anger would surface, mostly toward his own family.

Yet for six more years my mother would enjoy me, my hus-band, and our son.

THE DAY MY WHOLE LIFE ENDED

The day before my world fell apart, I was given one last time to be with my mother, one last time to remember every little detail about her, one last time to feel her presence and know her love.

Thank God I listened to a feeling I had that day.

It was normal for my husband and me to be loaded down with work. We had more appointments than time to fit them all in. We had hectic days and nonstop nights. We had an eighteen-month-old son, and we struggled with schedules. On this particular morning I hurried to get dressed and was quickly cleaning up the dishes in the sink. I had decided to drop my son at my mother's on my way to our office. Then something funny happened to me while I was standing at the sink. I stood there and had a sudden impulse to call my mother and go on a picnic. It was so strong, I could not ignore it. My husband would think I had gone haywire. We both relied heavily on each other, and real estate was crazy with excitement this summer. Rates were down, and buyers and sellers were everywhere. We were making money as fast as we could sell homes. I was really in my element. Yet I could not resist this feeling.

My husband walked into the kitchen and I shared my thoughts with him. To my surprise, he urged me to go. "Go ahead, honey," he said. "Change your clothes and call your mom. I'll handle things, don't worry." Within the hour she was at my house with a big black umbrella, a thermos of lemonade, and an old worn blanket. We were off . . . and there was not a cloud in the sky. As I look back on that day, I could not have created a more perfect memory.

We drove to the lake. My mother and my son played in the

sand for a long while. They went for ice cream, and eventually when he tired, she patted his little bottom and he fell sound asleep under the old black umbrella.

We talked about everything and nothing. At one point, my mother brought up my brother Bruce. "I wonder where he's been, honey. I wonder why we haven't heard from him in months." I was so glad I hadn't seen him, I thought. "He's done nothing but cause us trouble," I told her. I wanted to change the subject. It was too nice a day to think about him. I was happy. She was so happy just to be with me. We had never done this. As the afternoon wore on, it came time to leave. I felt so good inside.

We started to pack up, and I glanced across the grassy knoll. There was my husband, walking toward us and carrying a big brown basket. "Thought I'd surprise you girls," he said. "Brought you a little picnic dinner." A sudden urge told him we might be here, and he'd stopped at the store and bought chicken, potato salad, grapes, cheese, and dessert. He'd even doubled back home to grab a bottle of white wine.

We were laughing because I teased him, saying it was the last bottle we had and should be saving it for a special occasion. My mother smiled and said how much she enjoyed herself. "Could we do this more often?" she asked. An already perfect day now turned into a wonderful evening. "Tomorrow I'll baby-sit for you kids," she said, "and we'll have a nice dinner at my place when you get through working."

She loved planning ahead, especially if she was part of the plans. Things should have turned out just her way, but they never did.

The following morning I had all kinds of signals that something was very wrong. I ignored them. I know now that I was not supposed to go over to my mother's house that morning, no matter what. As I readied myself to leave for work, I ran out to start my car. It was dead. My husband would have to drop me off at our real estate office; it was his day off, so that could work. Now that I think back, much later in the day, my car started with no outside help. Could this have been divine intervention at the time? That morning I had a strange premonition something very bad was going to happen. I had this feeling from the moment I awoke, and I tried to ignore it.

At my office I proceeded to get my morning coffee and settle down at my desk. I was going to call my mother to check in, as I had been doing for years.

Before I called her, before I sat down, I looked outside and thought, "Another perfect day, too nice to be working. At least one of us can be outside." My mother had probably already been working in her garden since early morning. She loved summer so much; she just loved working out in her yard. Her roses and all her pretty flowers got her best attention in these early hours. So often, I would surprise her and find her down on her knees weeding and working in the yard, late into the day. She would look up and smile. "Hi, honey, can I get you something to eat?"

My husband and I loved just going over and sitting on the patio. Her backyard was thick with trees and flowers. She had a pretty stone birdbath and little statues of cherubs and animals scattered throughout the bushes and shrubbery. There were so many evenings when the fragrant smell of rosebushes mixed in with whatever she was grilling at the time. For it was always more inviting at her home than our own. So often, after a long day in real estate, we were just too tired to go home and cook.

Lately, we managed to spend more and more of our evenings with her. She was always pleading with us to bring our son over to her house. "Leave him here," she would say. "He's fine with me. You kids go on to a movie." She was so tender and loving with our little boy. As active as he was, he never wore her out. She would pull him around and around the patio in the old red wagon she had bought at a garage sale.

My husband had planned to drop our son off at her house that morning.

Now as I look back, it was divine intervention. For after he dropped me at the office, he was supposed to drive over to my mother's, drop off our son, then do his errands. Afterward he was to pick me back up at the office. For some strange reason, on the way over to her house, he changed his mind.

He never went there.

I dialed my mother's number. She was supposed to answer the phone as she always did every morning when I called. This morning Bruce answered the phone instead. "Where had he come from?" I thought. An alarm when off inside me. I recalled past violent episodes. "What do you want?" he demanded. His tone of voice was so menacing. I felt such fear immediately build within me. I asked to talk with my mother right away. Before he let me speak to her, I felt a sudden sick feeling growing in my stomach. It was the kind of feeling you get in a "near miss" when you narrowly avoid a car accident. When I heard his voice on the telephone, I instinctively wanted to drop everything I was doing, use someone's car, and drive immediately over to my mother's house. Everything in me cried out to do just that, but I didn't. After I spoke with my mother, she reassured me in a quiet tone that everything was fine. We would plan to meet at her house for lunch. At that moment, my sales manager came up from behind, waiting impatiently for me to get off the phone. He wanted me to go look at a new listing in the area. I felt so torn. I thought, "I can always borrow a car . . . run over there when I get back, it won't take that long. . . ."

I looked at the clock on the wall. The time read 9:05 A.M.

I thought about all the feelings racing around inside my head. I looked at the beautiful sunny day outside. It's my imagination, I thought. Nothing's wrong here; everything will be fine. I'll go over for lunch just as we planned. I'll sit out on her patio, we'll have lunch together, there's nothing to be worried about.

I remember the entire day as if in slow motion.

I had just come back from looking at a house. As I walked into my office, everyone looked at me as though they'd seen a ghost. They just stared at me. My husband was standing in the back of the office. He started walking toward me. I recall he was dressed in khaki shorts and a white golf shirt. His reddish brown hair was matted down, and his eyes were moist and red. He appeared to have been crying. I stopped midway in my office and froze. I watched his tall, slim frame come walking toward me, and I cried out for our son.

My husband walked over to me and gently put his arm around my shoulder. Everyone in the office kept staring at us. "He's okay," he said. "He's at the neighbor's. He's just fine. . . . It's your mom, Barb. . . . It's your mom, honey. She died this morning."

It was so strange at first, because he told me this in such a gentle manner. I immediately thought she'd had a heart attack. Thank God I was with her, I thought! Thank God for yesterday . . . we had that picnic. I was so relieved. But the mind is quick to remember. It never, ever stops thinking. "But wait . . . didn't my brother answer the phone when I called for her? Why, why didn't he help her?" I asked. "He was there, I know, I talked to him! I talked to Bruce before I talked to Mother! She was going to make him some breakfast. We were going to come over there for lunch! . . . We were going to sit out on her patio! . . ."

My husband was grabbing my arm harder now. He was telling me we had to go. He would explain everything to me out in the car. But when I mentioned my brother, I saw his eyes change. He was squeezing my arm too tightly, he was pulling on me, his own eyes filling with anger and tears. I had to sit down right away. I couldn't think straight. I didn't want my thoughts to move one second further. . . . I had to write my ads for Sunday, I told my husband. I can't leave yet! I can't leave here. I have to get my open houses ready. Everything had to stay normal, it all had to stay normal—couldn't anyone see this? I couldn't, . . . oh God . . . I couldn't stand to let my mind even consider the next thought. Please, please . . . God, no! Not my brother . . . not him! He couldn't have done something like this. . . .

Could he?

My mother had been murdered at nine twenty-five in the morning. Just twenty minutes after I had spoken with her on the phone. The gruesome scene of how he left her will stay with me forever. She still had some of the pink curlers left in her hair when the coroner arrived. Out in the yard, other pink curlers were found underneath a pine tree in front of her house where she lay dead. The rest were with the ninety-seven pieces of blood-soaked evidence taken from the crime scene.

While I waited for the trial, the following two years were one endless nightmare from which I could never awake.

Going over his case history with an attorney, I saw how my brother's drug problem had escalated into a full-fledged horror story. Now, looking back, I see that this had weighed heavily on my marriage as well. Still, I had no idea just how much this tragedy would soon engulf my whole family, causing me to take on the entire court system in a fight to keep my brother locked up. The sadness, fear, and depression were to shackle me down for a very long time.

On the charge of first-degree murder, my brother was found "not guilty by reason of insanity."

To this day he sits, waiting, in a state maximum-security hospital, appealing every so often for his release.

The trial took its toll on me personally, as well. It also took its toll on my marriage.

A lot of people might say to me, I had a good husband, a good career, two beautiful children. (Our second child, a *girl*, had been born one year after my mother's death.) I appeared to be leading a charmed life, even after my mother's brutal murder. Why, then, would I deliberately choose a divorce? This is where I learned a big lesson. By definition, no one is prepared for the "unexpected." When you're hit by "unexpected tragedy," that is when you are called upon to use your highest tools of awareness to deal with the struggle and dig yourself out. Unfortunately, the tools from my childhood were not healthy, healing tools. My husband and I didn't have proper tools to build a healthy marriage and, above all, overcome any tragedy.

I had created my own married life as one would create a movie or a play. I had handpicked my husband. He appeared to come from a good, sound family. I pushed him into the real estate profession. After all, my father had been a top sales producer before his life went down the drain. He'd been pushy and manipulative. He'd always bragged about how easy being a salesman was. Could this have had anything to do with my choice of careers? I was used to control and manipulation, wanting things my way—then resenting the outcome. Subconsciously, I resented the fact I could manipulate a man who should have had his own power.

Often, my husband and I enjoyed a marriage of convenience. He was raised with a firm, cold, distant hand. I was comfortable caretaking in my own way. I learned from my mother. After my father's death, my mother had gone right from caretaking my father into caretaking my brother Bruce, whenever he was around. When he wasn't there, she'd turned to me. My husband and I had spent many a day and evening eating and camping at her house while she waited on us hand and foot. She'd loved playing nursemaid to our every need. My husband loved the attention, and I'd needed her so very much.

For five years before our son was born, we'd worked night and day selling real estate. I was comfortable with extremes. My mother was lonesome with no one around and would do anything to have us with her as much as possible. We'd all met one another's needs at the time. Who doesn't want to be taken care of?

There are so many pieces to the puzzle of making a marriage work. I had been desperate to live happily ever after. I now see so vividly the holes, so many ways our own marriage was doomed from the start. For the most part, my husband and I didn't have a spiritual relationship. Oh, together we found a way to talk. Yet we had devised a system of immediate gratification. If there was a lull in the marriage, we brought in more people. If we were bored, we bought something new. If we needed a change of scenery, we took a trip. If problems arose, we took another trip. We were making plenty of money, and we spent it too. We bought one property after another; this seemed to bring me security. Very seldom did we fight. This was far too scary for me. I had seen too much of this in my own childhood. We just ignored uncomfortable issues that needed to be dealt with, thinking they would somehow just go away.

If things got bad between us, I preferred to run away—get in my car, take a long drive, lock myself in my room, go to the store, anything to avoid confronting our own marital problems. At the very end of our marriage, I still had not dealt with my grief from the murder of my mother. There was one thing I was convinced of, however: there had not been a good support system between me and my husband.

I remember saying to my marriage counselor, "I just can't understand how it got to this. We never, ever fought."

"You never talked either," said the counselor. "You both lived together in the same house—together, separately."

Often people think that if an affair takes place in a marriage, one of the partners will blame the breakup exclusively on the affair. For years I felt I was to blame for having an affair. I was trying to get my husband's attention and hurt him for past deeds done. This was very unhealthy thinking on my part. Now I believe an affair only adds insult to an already severe injury. By the time an affair takes place, unbelievable damage has accumulated and trust has been destroyed.

My husband had many good qualities, yet I had allowed him to take some of my power. His nature was more intimidating when we were alone. He was never physically abusive of me, yet his tone of voice and his aloof, distant manner, at the times I needed him the most, would be the shutoff valve in our relationship. Our future happiness was doomed, for this valve would remain closed. I became filled with resentment toward him. We never found a comfort level for communicating. We set up our own boundaries from the start; I guess we thought love would come later. Now I finally know that you need the right tools and a forgiving heart daily in order to make marriage work. Above all, however, there must be communication, affection, and respect.

I look back on what I had done and realize now I acted out of fear, fear to face the truth each day. I honestly believe at that point in time, my resource for handling problems in any healthy manner at all was depleted—I had nothing to go on. I have since written my former husband letters of apology in hopes he will forgive me, and I have asked for guidance and know I forgive myself.

My own story is a recipe for living life using all of the ingredients included in this manual. The tragic experience of losing my own mother at the hand of my brother taught me a powerful lesson in love and forgiveness. As I watched my own body fall apart at the seams, I learned out of sheer desperation how to heal my being from a holistic approach. I learned a great deal about good health. Little by little, I started feeling better than I had felt in years. I found my own spirituality when I waved an internal flag and cried out to God for help. My personal power evolved out of a desire, determination, and discipline to find a new way to live. With discipline each day, life became less depressing and easier to deal with. My own family gave me my greatest lesson.

My hardest task was being able to find forgiveness for my own brother, who murdered our mother. Forgiveness . . . the one ingredient taking the longest time, the hardest work, and the most effort.

When it came to balance in my work, I thought, hadn't I always worked? What did "workaholic" mean? I had found myself a good respectable profession. I was a real estate agent. I had sold homes for many years. I knew what I was supposed to do with my life—or did I? What had I really come here to do? What had I sacrificed? How did I balance each day?

Throughout my life, I had always feared not making enough money. When I discovered my real purpose in life, my true life's work, I got my greatest reward. Money came and the fear left.

With this book, I share the twelve ingredients for a recipe for living, a recipe so simple I sometimes smile when I think of how long it took to learn. We all have painful hardships that keep us from finding joy. I sincerely hope this recipe will help you find your way out, your path, and a new awareness.

We can change our life one day at a time with a disciplined recipe.

Everything that happens to us in life, happens for a reason. I know that you are probably thinking, "That is not fair!" This is true. Yet who ever said life was fair?

I believe we go through life with blinders on. We think all that is in front of us is "truth." Actually, all that is in front of us is a mirror—a mirror reflecting what our own reality is telling us. This is not always truth.

Everything that happens to us every day gives us much-needed opportunities for internal growth. The tools we utilize to deal with life are the key to growing.

Every person needs direction to get to a given place. If we wish to grow and go forward in truth and light and with a purpose, we need a map. We need direction. We need a recipe.

The Life Awareness Manual offers a recipe for living life with balance, forgiveness, and letting go. Yes, it presents a challenge.

Yet in turn it provides you with valuable tools for dealing with personal pain. Every day you encounter new problems that bring with them personal pain. Situations that seemingly put you between a rock and hard place. Whether you know it or not, each and every person has asked for specific lessons for personal growth and self-awareness. Each of us is given our own set of lessons to learn, and not judge.

I feel *The Life Awareness Manual* is a miracle book. It promises you that the answers lie within you.

It offers a "quick fix" for emotional and spiritual problems, a road map to follow each and every day of the year as you travel down your own spiritual path of awareness. I hope this book can help guide you to enlightenment and learning. Learn how to deal with setbacks and sadness. For there is no reason to stay stuck. Keep moving.

Keep growing.

This book is a learning tool that focuses on light. Light is all around us. Light is energy. Light is within each and every one of us. When you turn the light on, you see things much more clearly.

Each chapter of this book has a separate ingredient to learn, a concept to be chewed, swallowed, and digested. To use each part of the recipe, you will need complete discipline, discernment, and detachment from old ways and old habits. When we keep doing the same things, the same things keep happening.

This book will help you become aware. Giving you guidance each day, it will show you how and where to tap into your own personal power. When the light goes on, you will feel friendly toward yourself. You will have a reunion with your conscience, and life will feel safe. There are twelve parts to the recipe: love, health, family, forgiveness, discipline, work, money, relationships, marriage, relaxation, spirituality, and rules for living. With balance in these areas, we are in alignment with the universe.

You can find peace in life.

The tools in this manual are guided tools to use each day. The recipe takes courage, discipline, and forgiveness—constantly starting over.

There is no one else for you to rely on, no place else for you to turn to, nowhere else to go except within. Within your own self lie all the answers. Ask for help and listen for direction.

I believe stress is the single most destructive factor in a person's life.

Going within yourself is the single most effective way to deal with it.

You have the power now and the ability to change negatives into positives. You will always receive what it is you want. However, most of our wants have been on a lower, superficial level. This book will help you adopt a higher degree of self-awareness, which will help you tune into your deepest, most authentic self. The principles are easy to understand, but you will need discipline and a clear intent to incorporate them into your life. To obtain the maximum benefit from each chapter, I suggest you read and reread each of them several times.

Chapter 1

LOVE

*The only real thing
in life is love.*

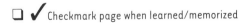
☐ ✓ Checkmark page when learned/memorized

1st Ingredient: Love

*"I believe in unconditional love,
love so great nothing can destroy it."*

Throughout my life, I searched for love. My family disappointed me when there was no love there. I looked for love in a boyfriend and found my heart broken many times. I tried to find love in marriage and realized more than once that a husband could not give me what I did not have inside. I looked for love in all kinds of people. When I could not find it there, I replaced the void love left with work.

Long bouts with liquor replaced long, lonely nights.

It never dawned on me to look to myself for love. How could I do this? How could I find something in me I never knew I possessed? How could I create love within me when I was filled with bitterness? Where was I to begin when I had spent the better part of my life searching, starting over, and hurting so much?

The "Love" chapter can change you greatly, if you allow it to. Begin to trust in the 1st Ingredient of this recipe, and you will see how I did this. You will begin to understand just how important you are. Whether you believe this or not, you have a special purpose here.

The easiest way I can explain love to you is by switching on a lamp. Notice how warm and good the light feels. See how it erases darkness. A ray of light allows you to see clearly. You must believe there is an internal light residing deep within you. When you turn on your own internal light, you ignite a flame that burns forever. For love lives inside your being.

Before you can love anything else in the world, you first must be able to love yourself. Love for yourself can happen in a breath. Here is the way it works.

Take a very deep breath then exhale saying, "I love myself, I love myself . . ." At first, it sounds hollow. Are you curious? Do you know whether you truly love yourself? Say these words: "I can love myself—I will love myself—I do love myself." Look in the mirror and repeat this.

Nothing you have done or have not done makes any difference now. You are right where you are supposed to be in your own life. Everything has happened to you thus far to teach you lessons. You are ready NOW *to start making progress for you, today.*

Perhaps you feel you are loved. Love comes from a father, mother, spouse, or friend. Ah, but is this genuine, permanent love? What happens when a spouse divorces? What happens when a parent dies? What happens when a friend goes away—and never calls again? Where is the love then?

Perhaps you feel you are unloved. There is anger inside of you. Many parts of you fill with resentment. Fear and loneliness seem to follow you wherever you go. This is due to a lack of love in your life.

You probably wonder how I learned to love myself and depend on God. I believe God uses defeat and failure to bring us to an awareness of who we really are.

It was very simple. I learned to be quiet more. I took time for myself, I turned off all the noise and spent time alone with myself. I focused on the simple things in life . . . the trees, the birds, the sky. I took long walks. I so wanted to get rid of the fear and loneliness inside of me.

I wanted to know love and feel love for myself, but I did not know how to do this. On days I walked or spent time alone at home, I tried talking silently to God, to the universe around me. Little by lit-

tle, I began to feel better about life. Yet still I felt sorry for myself. One day while sitting on my front steps consumed by fear and sadness, I put my hands together and prayed for my life to be different.

Suddenly, I heard a beautiful voice talking to me. An angelic voice telling me, "You are not alone. Life is for learning lessons every single day. There will be lessons to learn as long as you are alive." I sat there staring in disbelief for a long moment. Then I walked over to my car and sat in it for a long while. I had prayed for help. Could this be it? What if life was just about learning lessons? I was now aware of a peaceful presence inside of me that humbled me greatly. I was full. I was content. I was at peace.

Take your time with this chapter. Start slowly. Don't be afraid to have enough self-love to let go of things that aren't good for you. Tell yourself "I can—I can. To know love, feel love, and give love, I must first learn to love myself." Repeat this in front of a mirror.

Let go of old anger. Tell yourself, "I forgive myself for how I have been in the past. I handled life the only way I knew how then." Try to say to yourself, "Look at what life has dealt me so far. Things happened in my past to teach me lessons. Did I learn? If I let go of feelings that hurt me, I can start to feel real love."

Feel the warm rays of love build inside of you.

Years ago I started doing this, and my life changed in amazing ways. The only way I could learn to love myself was to sit quietly for a certain period of time, perhaps twenty minutes or more, focus quietly on my breath, and begin to calm down. I tell myself, "Nothing is so important that I need to let go of calm. I am in control, and no person, event, or situation, will upset me. All events in my life happen to give me lessons to learn from."

I go easy on myself. It is understood now. Love exists and so does God. The one word that has the power to save me from myself . . . Love.

Key to Ingredient 1: I can love God. I can love myself.

To know love, feel love, and give love, I must first learn to love myself.

At certain times love is like a meteorite; it hits swift and hard, when you least expect it.

There is no possible way to saddle, capture, or harness love. I can only feel, give, and experience love. I will love myself.

Love is appreciated much more when it is felt first for oneself, so I will learn to love myself.

One does not need to be in love to feel love.

Love has various stages and periods of growth.

Unconditional love is always the right love.

Love is anticipated first before any other emotion. Whether you listen to your higher self is another story. It takes discipline.

Love is accelerated and expanded to the breadth and height of your own awareness.

I cannot give love if love is not in my heart for myself. I love myself unconditionally.

Love is always the true leader.

Love is like the wind. Never try to guess which direction it will suddenly decide to take.

❑ ✔ Checkmark page when learned/memorized

Love is always more when I give it first before all other things in my life.

Unconditional love lets nothing stand in its way. Unconditional love removes ego, pride, and fear.

Love is outstanding in every argument and is considered the silent victor.

Love proves any hero a fool and every fool a hero. Sometimes love will fool you.

Love does not deal spades but always the ace of hearts. We learn from what we are dealt.

Love is never a battle; love will win every war.

Love dictates no timetables for position of merit, yet love is merciful, patient, and forgiving every time.

Love is always felt deeply within the heart.

The true test of love is discipline for what is right to do, no matter how much it hurts.

Love holds hands with every manner of man, woman, and child if they but give it theirs.

Love is the least painful if one can forgive. Forgiveness takes courage, every single day.

Love keeps all people eternally young.

❏ ✔ Checkmark page when learned/memorized

When I feel love for myself, I will go easier on myself. I accept Lessons to Learn in my life.

When I feel true love for another, I will always want what is *right* for both of us, regardless. Even if this means walking away.

How to know if I do love myself? I ask myself whether I feel sad, indifferent, or peaceful, day in and day out.

Love realizes that all things, ways, and people may change in a breath, but love for oneself never gives up, gives in, or dies.

Love leads many men, women, and children to the greatest awareness of all—truth.

To truly love is to truly live in the light.

Love lessens no person.

Love may prefer to sit quietly in the background and watch. Forgive and trust that all things work out for the good of all.

Why love? To live life at its very fullest!

Love decides to forgive every minute, every hour, and every day.

Love cannot mend a broken heart unless it lets go of pride, ego, and anger.

When you fall in love, there is an uncompromising feeling to always want the best for the other person, whether you remain the intended or not.

Love permits and practices patience.

❏ ✓ Checkmark page when learned/memorized

Love can wait a lifetime and can take a lifetime to be found.

Love prefers to be found in all ways.

Let go of all hatred, ill will, and anger. Love will find a way to replace, repair, and reward you beyond your wildest dreams.

There is only love . . . all else is an illusion.

Prayer will help me to find love and know and learn about my true self.

There are no mistakes in love, only lessons to learn. Every day I receive more lessons.

I will attract my idea of love at the level of awareness I am at, or am willing to grow to.

Love is a leader when it comes to forgiveness, understanding, and compassion for others.

Love lets the sun in. Love manifests itself.

Love for myself is what saved me from myself. I am vulnerable to love.

It took me a very long time to learn not to search for love, but to love myself first. To be at peace and truly start to know myself, this is the start of a new beginning in my life.

True love for God and oneself makes a true leader out of any person.

❏ ✔ Checkmark page when learned/memorized

The right person is available for each person if you lift your awareness level.

To be aware of who is truly right for each of us, we must learn to be quiet, loving, and open for ten to fifteen minutes of each and every day.

Brief moments of solitude can bring great feelings of love.

When I learn to love myself, I will begin a remarkable journey.

If I love myself and all others, I will know that I am here on a specific mission. My job is to spend the least amount of my life getting to this point!

There are no accidents or mistakes. Every person is meant to be here. Love is in everything.

Each person has a purpose. Each person has love somewhere deep inside.

I find the light within myself when I find the love for myself.

Love predicts, promises, and promotes healing of all kinds in all people.

I love myself, and I will learn to know myself and become more aware daily.

There are two parts of me: my lower self and my higher self. My higher self loves my lower self regardless.

I love my mother, father, brother, and sister. I picked them before I arrived here. I can grow strong and loving from family experiences.

I will love everyone unconditionally. It doesn't matter what they have done. I forgive them and love them from a distance. I don't even have to see them. This removes the dis-ease from within me.

Love leads to forgiveness. Love and forgiveness are attributes of the strong. Love heals my entire being.

I say a love prayer: *"The light of God surrounds me, the love of God enfolds me, the power of God protects me, and the presence of God watches over me. Wherever I am, God is and all is well."* This is the greatest love and protection one can ever acquire.

I appreciate the love someone gives, sends, and feels for me. I accept all the love I am given.

I send out love every hour of the day. The more I think loving thoughts, the more love comes directly back to help me heal.

I thought I knew love, was in love, and felt love until the universe tested me.

True love only knows, speaks, and lives the truth. Love tries hard to be kind.

For every person there is someone to love. If I but look, and listen to my inner guidance and my inner voice, I find peace.

❏ ✓ Checkmark page when learned/memorized

A Relationship Test

1. Left column: What is most important to me? Rank 1 to 12.
2. Right column: How satisfied (in these areas) am I with my partner? Rate your partner 1 to 10. (Perfect is 10)
3. Compare answers with your partner and discuss them.

THE MOST IMPORTANT TO ME   THE MOST YOU SATISFY ME

SHARING EXPERIENCES
Sharing experiences of life
_____ (e.g., music, nature, art, theater, dance, and movies). _____

COMMUNICATING
Being honest, trusting, truthful, and loving;
giving constructive feedback; positive confrontation,
_____ telling each other how you feel. _____

EMOTIONS
Having an awareness of and sharing each other's
feelings; the touching of the innermost selves of
_____ two human beings, sensitivity to each other. _____

CREATIVITY
Helping each other to grow and be caregivers
(not caretakers) of each other; "complementing
_____ each other"; bringing out the best. _____

SEXUALITY
Enjoying sensual-emotional satisfaction; the
experience of sharing the physical merging of
_____ two people; pleasing each other physically. _____

❏ ✓ Checkmark page when learned/memorized

CRISIS
Standing together in the major and minor tragedies
in life; closeness in coping with problems and
pain together; being close.

_____   _____

SPIRITUALITY
Growing together with God, the meaning of life;
religious experiences together.

_____   _____

CONFLICT
Facing and struggling with day-to-day differences;
fighting, resolving conflict, and *above all*
making up.

_____   _____

RECREATION
Sharing experiences of fun, sports, hobbies,
recreation; giving each other positive energy;
doing fun things together.

_____   _____

INTELLECTUAL PURSUITS
Sharing the world of ideas; a mutual respect for
each other's intellectual capacities
(reading, discussing, studying).

_____   _____

WORK
Going to work daily. Is work more important than
my partner? What is my true purpose in life?
Am I happy at work? Is my partner?

_____   _____

COMMITMENT
Striving for togetherness derived from dedication
to each other and a common value system.
How have we made a commitment
to each other? Do we have goals?

_____   _____

☐ ✓ Checkmark page when learned/memorized

I love where I am in life. I am here for a reason. I learn the lesson before I attempt to move on.

There is a reason for life: love. I just can't stop believing that I am given all I need.

Love always lets the light in the darkest room.

Love sets me straight with those around me—those against me and those who know me best.

Love survives all lifetimes.

True love lets the couple play and giggle together as children, make mad passionate love together as lovers, and counsel each other as a parent or a teacher. This is known as a brilliant balance, one that takes lifetimes to achieve.

Love is always open to another way, another day, come what may. Love is all there ever is.

Love sees me through all physical and emotional difficulty.

With unconditional love in my life, I am no longer bound by earthly limitations—I can spread my wings and fly . . .

❑ ✔ Checkmark page when learned/memorized

Chapter 2

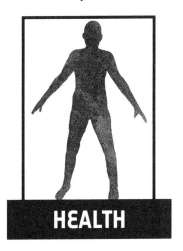

HEALTH

Heal the spirit and the mind will grow;
heal the mind and the body will follow.

☐ ✔ Checkmark page when learned/memorized

2nd Ingredient: Health

*"I believe being healthy means that body,
mind, and spirit are in balance."*

For a great part of my life, I took my health for granted. I didn't
think about whether I felt good or bad because of what I put into my
body, or how I treated it. I always thought the way I felt each day de-
pended on the kind of mood I was in. My moods decided how
healthy I stayed.

Throughout most of my adult years, I drank a large amount of
wine and many vodka tonics during the week. I ate cheeseburgers
and french fries and drank Coke. I craved chocolate. I smoked cigarettes. I thought nothing of it, as all my friends did the same. I considered antidepressants for my daily struggles. It was simply too scary
to face life with a clear head.

But regardless of how much I continued to anesthetize myself, the
depressed feelings stayed. I could not imagine a life without smoking,
without liquor, without junk food. I had watched my parents and
relatives resort to chemicals to relax and unwind, for party and pleasure. A life without them appeared boring, mundane, senseless. I re-
fused to admit I was nervous most of the time. I suffered from
anxiety attacks. My depression was constant, and I had trouble
sleeping nights.

One day a young girl came up to me while I was speaking at a
high school. She held an earlier edition of my book in her hand,
telling me, "It changed my whole life. I can't believe how I used to

eat and live. I had no idea what 'holistic health' meant until reading your book." She'd been putting chemicals, junk food, and cigarette smoke into her body. She said her family never ate together and there was lots of junk food, cigarettes, and liquor consumed at home. She told me her body had begun to break down. I knew what she was talking about, because I had been there too. I had been hurting all over, and wasn't even forty yet. She told me it was hard to study at home, because her parents fought a lot, the house was a mess, and no one seemed to care. She was all worn out at seventeen years of age and still needed to deal with daily problems of her own.

I continued telling her of a pain I felt in my chest whenever I smoked cigarettes. After I drank soft drinks or coffee, I felt wired up. When I ate cheeseburgers and french fries, I became clogged up. I was always worried about going to the bathroom. I turned to health books to educate myself. I found out that fiber, fruit, and water kept me regular throughout the week. I began to clean out the junk food in my life. It took a while, but I quit eating red meat, pork, and chicken, because I believe they are loaded with cancer-causing chemicals.

She stood silent and listened. Then she told me she chose to live with an aunt because her own family did not want to be healthy. The recipe in this book has continued to give her guidance, and she has found peace.

The great number of people who wrote to me convinced me of how much we all need a healthy road map for daily living. The continuing letters convinced me that I should do a revised edition of the book. Many different sources were now convincing me that it was not just the food I ate, it was how I took care of my body and what my belief system was that was important.

Holistic health means a belief in a balanced body, mind, and spirit. In other words, eating good, thinking good, and praying and talking to God. The more healthfully I ate, the easier it was to deal with life, handle daily problems, and be prepared for the unexpected.

I was determined to heal myself without more chemicals, drugs, and cigarettes. I started by going for long walks and swimming three times a week. The first thing I noticed was that my depression began to lift almost immediately! I have to admit, things started slowly when it came to changing my diet. I didn't give up all junk food, but I started taking responsibility each day for what I put into my body. I made lots of fruits, vegetables, and salads the centerpiece of my diet.

Just about every day now I find some way to get exercise. I know thirty minutes of exercise releases endorphins into my body, which are natural stress reducers. If the weather is bad, I can always walk the malls! Some days I walk; some days I swim; some days I ride a bike. While I exercise, I pray and meditate. I talk and listen to God.

Daily prayer gives me that added strength. I pray at different times of the day. Sometimes I pray while I'm driving my car. I have learned to listen to inspirational tapes. I meditate daily, clearing away all thoughts, the garbage, paying attention to my breath, learning how to pay closer attention to my internal higher self. Every day I find at least twenty minutes just for myself.

I eat breakfast now, a meal I routinely skipped, telling myself I was too busy. I do not drink coffee. Often, I eat oatmeal and drink various herbal teas with a piece of whole-wheat toast.

I eat salad and soup for lunch and eat light at night. Lots of brown rice, whole-wheat pasta, soups, salads, fruits, nuts, raw vegetables, brown bread, and vegetarian enchiladas. I choose whole grain and organic foods. The list is endless once you start. For a treat, I mix candied almonds with raisins—wonderful! I drink six to *eight glasses of purified water daily and take lots of vitamins—most of the time. (We all slip up now and then.) Just start over. I love to read anything I can find on health and nutrition. For relaxation, I find spiritual books and biographies of interesting people.*

My friends have changed for the better. People who pulled me down in the past have disappeared. Now my friends and I share common interests. Most of the people I know now don't hang out in bars. They seldom drink liquor. I try to go to bed before eleven each night and rise around seven. I don't talk on the phone a lot; I watch little television. I read fewer newspapers. I try not to get emotionally involved in how the media sensationalizes sad events. These events are other people's lessons. I pray for them and move on.

I try to remain calm each day. I thank God for giving me the discipline to start my day. If other people rile me, I take a deep breath, ask for guidance, and know this is one of my lessons being played out to see how I will handle it. I continue to pray for others and for peace all around me.

No more chemicals, soft drinks, cigarettes, drugs, or alcohol. I rarely eat junk food or fast foods. How do you feel about this?

I believe a lot of sickness comes from dis-ease—not feeling good about oneself and others. Illness is a great teacher.

It's ironic to say this, but I feel younger than I did fifteen years ago. I look better. I can accomplish more things now because I have the tools for good health. I feel so much better about myself.

Key to Ingredient 2: Daily I exercise, eat healthfully, and evolve spiritually.

For total health, one needs physical, mental, emotional, and spiritual balance.

Complete health is not just physical awareness, but spiritual and mental awareness as well.

Heal the spirit and the mind will grow.

Heal the mind and the body will follow.

Heal the heartbreak and love will be present and overflowing.

Learn to go quietly within yourself. Quiet the mind. Quiet the voices. Take several deep breaths in a row; in through the nose and out through the mouth. Be absolutely quiet. Don't talk within. Learn to be still and know.

I harvest all the good around me in others. I do not dwell on another person's negative qualities unless I have none of my own.

Be prepared each day to let go of yesterday.

I am aware of those around me who need my help, not my hindsight, every day. I refrain from all gossip.

I drink at least six to eight large glasses of water every day. I drink bottled water or use a water-purification system. (Thirty million tons of toxins have gone into the earth over the last thirty years.)

❏ ✓ Checkmark page when learned/memorized

Fiber cereal helps me stay regular. Poisons need to be eliminated on a daily basis. I eat lots of bran.

I start the morning with two large glasses of water and fifteen minutes of quiet and deep breathing.

To eat right, I begin today. I start by eliminating overprocessed white foods (white flour, white sugar, white bread, milk, and salt). I eat fruits, salads, vegetables, and legumes. I begin to feel lighter!

I discipline myself daily with the understanding that every piece of food or drink that goes into my mouth goes somewhere in my body. How and when does it come out?

I heal the inside by watching the outside forces around me. I use the inner sources of guidance as perpetual spiritual nourishment and peace. There is always peace deep within.

I try to eliminate greasy foods, chocolate, caffeine, nicotine, alcohol, drugs, soft drinks, and carbonated beverages (cause gas) from my diet. My body deserves healthy food.

I practice eliminating harmful, negative, and sad thoughts from all my thinking. When they pop in, I say, "I'm okay. I'm living in the light. I am light. I'm surrounded in light."

Disease is absolutely "dis-ease."

Hatred, anger, greed, and jealously may eventually find their way out of the person in a physical, painful sense. Stress can build like a time bomb.

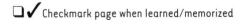 Checkmark page when learned/memorized

For a snack I eat almonds—they are good for me. I avoid peanuts. I prefer carob almonds and raisins.

Complete good health comes from balance in all areas of my being: *thinking right, eating right, and living right.*

I believe caffeine is very bad. I believe it contains tannic acid, which can cause cancer of the bladder. The stimulation is artificial and gets the adrenal glands going to get the caffeine out of the body! The body can't function normally. (Decaffeinated coffee has chemicals so potent I can take a rag and remove paint from furniture with it!) I drink herbal teas instead.

There are two thousand chemicals in cigarettes. Smoking causes cancer.

I read that butter, red meat, and dairy consumption are all associated with cancer, so I avoid them.

I seldom heat up oil. I use only cold-pressed oils for all of my cooking purposes, mostly olive oil.

I stay away from processed and dyed foods. Cheddar cheese has dark yellow dye. I believe cheese clogs the system.

All these foods are especially good: peaches, plums, apricots, prunes, almonds, kidney beans, lima beans, cherries, sweet potatoes, lentils, sprouts, and (purified) water.

I believe meat is extremely hard to digest. I prefer vegetables, nuts, and salads. The average thirty-five-year-old male has five pounds of undigested meat in his bowels.

❏ ✔ Checkmark page when learned/memorized

I drink lots of water every day.

Water is the major component of the blood (more than 80 percent). Water nourishes every cell. It is vital to removing body poisons.

Lettuce, watermelon, broccoli, carrots, cabbage, and celery are all more than 90 percent water.

Other foods high in water and good for me are: cold whole-grain cereals, salads, boiled potatoes, bananas, apples, oranges, baked fish, and cooked oatmeal.

No matter what my age, if I can walk, I do it! I go outside for fifteen minutes to a half hour and take a walk or go to the park.

Part of my good health comes from thinking good thoughts.

After replacing meat in my diet, I feel much better. I eat brown rice and vegetables.

When I do not exercise, I become lethargic. I have a tendency to be sadder. Some sort of exercise heightens my awareness level. I work out for 30 minutes daily.

There was a time in my life when I was told that I was severely depressed and needed all kinds of antidepressants. Instead, I decided to supplement my diet with vitamin B, three times a day after each meal, plus I take B_{12}. I swim three times a week. It worked. The depression went away. I worked with my spiritual counselor to treat my depression.

❏ ✓ Checkmark page when learned/memorized

I also take vitamin E every day (800 mg) for better circulation and four doses of vitamin C (500 mg). I take kelp for my nerves, and garlic detoxifies my body. Evening primrose oil is wonderful for my cramps, hot flashes, and other female disorders.

I believe chamomile tea is a wonderful sleep aid. Acidophilus and megadophilus can help my entire immune system. I take black cohosh for hot flashes, stomach problems, and blood pressure. I take calcium daily. I can get all of these vitamins at any health food store.

Grains and beans contain protein.

I eat fish broiled and/or baked.

Natural foods are whole-grain breads, pastas, nuts, seeds, vegetables, fruits, beans, and fish.

Much commercial cow milk contains pesticides, steroids, herbicides, detergents, and antibiotics. Does your body need them?

Exercise blows the stress right out of my body—at least 30 minutes a day.

Many people with terminal diseases have helped heal themselves with powerful mental, living-in-the-light attitudes.

I drink only purified water. I believe our drinking water is a big source of problems. Chlorine is added to the water to cleanse it.

Every morning I start my day with two glasses of water (room temperature). I do deep breathing for three to five minutes. I

❏✔ Checkmark page when learned/memorized

close my eyes and try to say two meaningful prayers, beginning with "Thank you."

It took me thirty days of practice to change my cravings for my old addictions. I did this one day at a time. It works.

I do not use artificial sweeteners. I use honey and maple syrup and brown sugar if I have to.

No matter what my age, I avoid the foods, liquids, and chemicals that are bad for me. I watch how different I feel.

I used to eat fried foods, drink, and smoke all the time, and I was always *depressed.*

This is what I feel happens when people go to extremes:

Too many calories = obesity.

Too much sugar = tooth decay.

Too much fat = heart disease and cancer.

Too much alcohol = cancer.

Too much dairy = colon cancer.

Too much meat = prostrate cancer.

I stop concerning myself with what others think about me. I feel good about me.

Suicide is never an option for leaving life. What makes me think that the lessons I learn end here?

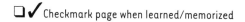 Checkmark page when learned/memorized

It is a proven fact that the immune system is supported much more strongly with large doses of self-love, laughter and positive attitudes, daily affirmations, and exercise.

Migraine headaches have been known to disappear with the removal of chocolate, cheese, tomatoes, MSG, nitrates, and milk from the diet.

There are more than one hundred million regular drinkers in the United States, and some estimates say that about 80 percent of adults are social drinkers and/or use other chemicals.

Alcohol is a central nervous system depressant. When I stopped drinking, my allergies cleared up completely!

There are 100 to 250 calories in most alcoholic drinks, not to mention 100 calories in a five-ounce glass of wine and 150 calories in an eight-ounce glass of beer.

Nothing ages a person more quickly than drinking and smoking and gossiping. There are empty calories in all of these.

Because I quit smoking, I will probably avoid heartburn, headaches, coughing, anxiety, depression, fatigue, allergies, heart disease, strokes, and many other side effects.

Breakfast choices for me include: oatmeal, Cream of Wheat, Red River Fiber One, All-Bran, granola, any kind of fruit, whole grain toast with honey, and herbal tea.

Sometimes I choose to fast on a small scale (three days on just juices and water). It has been very healing for me.

❏ ✔ Checkmark page when learned/memorized

Super good foods I eat are red and yellow peppers, carrots, strawberries, peaches, broccoli, cauliflower, beans, almonds, seeds, soybeans, whole grains, lettuce greens, oranges, lemons, grapefruit, onions, garlic, and parsley. Some fish are excellent sources of omega-3. Whole-wheat tacos are excellent with black beans and rice.

If you are eating too many carbohydrates, your energy will dip a few hours after you eat. Protein and fat, however, provide long-lasting energy.

Close your eyes and see a vision of yourself. See yourself active in life. See yourself cared for. See yourself eating well. Listen to your body and in return you will be rewarded with a healthy, long life.

I try hard to avoid high-fat foods such as the following: potato chips, butter, cheese, and deep-fried foods. I avoid whole milk and shortening and all the products with vegetable oils such as sunflower oil, corn oil, peanut oil, safflower oil, and margarine. Instead I use olive oil.

Regular bathing in a bathtub is essential to keeping my skin free from toxins as well as for relaxation and meditative affirmations.

Echinacea tea and drops act as an antibiotic, and the tea can help fight colds.

If I have a drug or chemical problem, one of the most wonderful things I can do is just to admit it to myself and say, "I have only this day to do differently."

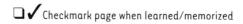 Checkmark page when learned/memorized

Addiction to drugs, chemicals, and alcohol has to do with the lower self, but everyone has a higher self as well.

Saunas, steam baths, and massages all purify the body through enhancing the elimination of toxins.

When I allow chemicals and drugs to enter my system, I allow a lower nature to take over my being. My awareness level drops.

If I eat light, I stay in the light and live in the light. I can stay youthful and more stress-free every day.

It is very important to retard aging and improve how the body functions to enhance elimination. Elimination detoxifies the body.

When my day is free of chemicals, drugs, and alcohol, I can finally have the ability to lift my awareness level and see reality, not an illusion of my true purpose in life.

Every person, regardless of age, has the right to good health. You can claim good health.

I let go of all things in the past. They are gone forever. I forgive all others.

The key to healthy living is letting go of the past that haunts us, forgiving those who have hurt us, and healing ourselves by getting in touch with our higher selves.

Healing ourselves begins with learning to be quiet, becoming aware of our inner selves, and developing spiritual awareness.

❏ ✔ Checkmark page when learned/memorized

How I think, what I eat, and who I am make up the recipe for "why I am."

It is not easy eating right. Every person's life revolves around food and drink.

I write down everything I eat and drink for one day. Everything I eat affects me one way or another.

When I drink juices like orange, cranberry, and grapefruit and eat cucumbers and lemons, I help flush my body poisons out.

Garlic is an aid against heart attacks because it contains an oil that interferes with the formation of blood clots. Garlic helps dissolve clots. I eat garlic daily = healthy heart and longer life.

When I feel a cold coming, I drink the following: eight to ten ounces of boiling water, to which I add the juice of half a fresh lemon, one tablespoon pure maple syrup, and a pinch of cayenne pepper. I sip this.

If I want gorgeous skin, I mix one tablespoon honey plus one teaspoon vinegar plus one egg white. I apply this to my skin, let it dry, then sponge it off gently.

Humor is healing. I can laugh at myself.

With a firm focus on creative and meaningful goals, a person's recovery from illness makes life worth fighting for.

The body has an unmistakable ability to self-heal. Each person can learn to "go within" and find the ability to heal.

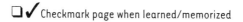 Checkmark page when learned/memorized

Willpower and attitude has so much to do with overcoming negative thought and disease in every living human being.

The body is always overhearing what the mind is thinking. You are constantly molding the kind of body that you want.

To be well, we must center on the fact that we are a combination of body, mind, and spirit. Each person is one energetic body of light.

Stress in our life brings an opportunity for positive change.

Each person's lifestyle must encompass balance. Some good food, quiet time, some laughter, a good friend, and love for oneself. I love myself and do what I love, and good health will follow.

Each day is the start of a new beginning of how I choose to eat. It will make a difference immediately. I start today and learn to eat in a better and more careful way.

The responsibility for good health lies within each person. We cannot go to a doctor and say "heal me." We have to learn to keep our energy high, to think and eat right. I let go of fear and negativity.

Eating better today will last through tomorrow, and little by little depression and stress will become less severe. Good health must encompass a healthy mind, body, and spirit.

Chapter 3

FAMILY

The family exists to teach us lessons.

❑ ✓ Checkmark page when learned/memorized

3rd Ingredient: Family

*"My family gave me many lessons to learn from,
for which I am grateful."*

I sat for the longest time trying to figure out a good way to start this chapter. It occurred to me that although I came from a troubled family background, I myself am unique in nature. There is only one of me. Never will I be ashamed of who I am again. I am who I am. I accept the fact that I asked to be born into my family to learn valuable lessons.

Within my family of origin, I had an abusive, alcoholic father who died at the ripe old age of fifty-two. My mother spent her life taking care of my father. She was murdered by the hand of my brother, who is now spending the rest of his life in a state hospital. My life was changed forever.

My family had many lessons to live through and opportunities to grow from. Everyone has something to overcome in a family. Everyone plays a significant role. Each person comes away a little bit wounded from some family situation. This ingredient helps heal.

We may not always notice how powerful a family upbringing is until we leave home to start a new life. Mannerisms, attitudes, emotional highs and lows—all are triggered by what we see and hear while growing up. A tremendous amount of guilt can be instilled. An abundance of anger can be perfectly programmed. Mood swings can be manipulated and acquired. Wonderful worlds waiting to be explored can be sadly closed off by parents who refuse to guide their own children positively.

What do I mean by this?

A middle-aged woman came up to me after I'd led a workshop on living a healthy life. "You know," she said, "my grandmother and my mother all died of breast cancer before the age of forty-five. I was terrified this would happen to me until I read your book. I have lived in fear for the better part of my life until only recently. I didn't know there was a better way to live. I had resigned myself that I would be dead before I was forty-five too. I have such a different outlook on life now." She said, "My grandma convinced my mother that would happen to her and my own mother told me that I would probably get it too. . . ." This woman had allowed her mother's gloomy predictions to define and shape her life. But her life is more than her fear of breast cancer. She learned that taking active steps to build health was more important than resigning herself to a deadly "family tradition."

Parents have an opportunity to mold children's characters. They incite courage or fear; they program confidence or guilt. They bring gladness or sadness. Many parents out there do a wonderful job. To those parents, I salute you. To the rest, I say, "Could this be a wake-up call?" Every one of us has a chance to start over.

If you are reading this now, you are meant to. Forgive yourself, your mate, and your own family. Look to your children as your teachers too.

When I began to work on myself, I spent endless hours analyzing why my life had to be so sad. Why did God have to punish me? Why did I have so many setbacks? Was I so terrible? The more I read, the more I learned. The more I learned, the more I opened up inside myself.

My body felt it had taken on several suits of armor, stacked one on top of the other. As I started to open up to new knowledge, the armor fell off, layer by layer. I kept reading the same thing over again.

"We pick the families we are born into so we can learn great lessons."

This part was the hardest for me. How could I have picked such a family? Why should I have to fix myself when others were to blame? As I learned more and more, I accepted the fact that anger and forgiveness run hand and hand. Without forgiveness, anger festers and grows, bitter infection spreads. Bodies often get diseased. We encounter long-term emotional setbacks. Why?

Pride, ego, and personality stand in the way.

We can say, "But you don't understand . . . you don't know how that hurt me, you don't know what that did to me. It wasn't my fault." This does not matter. What did we learn from the sadness, the anger, the hurt? What is the universe trying to teach us now? Can we let go, go forward?

We each have to look at who hurt us. Then, sometimes we must admit the hurt is bigger than anything we can handle on our own. Turn it over to a higher power and release the anger. Let go of pride, be the first to say, "It just doesn't matter anymore." If someone in your family continues to berate you, you may have to send him or her love from a distance. Leave that person alone. Stop dwelling on what happened. Refuse to discuss it with friends! One day I became so tired of all the anger stacked inside my being. I was tired of being angry. Tired of being loaded down with resentment. I wanted to learn to forgive.

I put my hands together and asked for help.

Then I drove myself down to the state hospital and asked the guard to let me in to see my brother. They ushered me into a tiny lit-

tle room, and brought him in. He had aged considerably, his hair was thinner, and his eyes were drained of color. Staring straight at the wall, he said nothing.

As I sat down, he looked over at me and then down at the floor. I could see part of his ear was missing—the guard told me he had cut it off with a pop can. My emotions went everywhere. I hated him. I was angry and sad at the same time. On instinct, I suddenly felt sorry for him. This was still my brother. Internally, I asked for courage and faith to replace my festering fear. For as long as I live, I will remember the look on his face when I spoke the words. "I forgive you," I said. "I forgive you for killing Mother."

Key to Ingredient 3: I asked for my family to learn valuable lessons from them.

A family can cement the future.

How fortunate is the family that grows together.

Within the family lie all the secrets of forgiveness.

Before I ever got here, I picked my family.

I love my parents and forgive them for everything, even if it's from a distance.

It is necessary to learn the value of patience from brothers and sisters.

Freedom within the family means becoming all that I can be. I keep my own identity and share the family pride of identity.

❑✓Checkmark page when learned/memorized

I was born into the family that I was given in order to learn valuable lessons that can, will, and should shape my life.

I love my family and forgive them when necessary. There are many lessons to be learned daily from my family.

I am patient with my mother and father. This helps them to see themselves for who they are.

The greatest gift one can give within the family is to feel with the heart.

The family that eats dinner, talks, and forgives together stays together.

Within the family lie many separate realities, yet one truth.

I stop analyzing my family and start appreciating my own worth.

I accept all that has happened within my family as past awareness and now look to the future as living the lessons learned.

I feel with my heart for my family.

To know my family is not to learn about why my family was the way they were, but rather to learn about how I can become aware of who I am.

The family is free when it builds a bridge that replaces a wall.

The amazing mother is one who knows how to nurture, guide, and gently take a back seat.

❑ ✔ Checkmark page when learned/memorized

The fun-loving father is one who can enjoy and still feel romance for the mother.

A family builds relationships today for the children's future.

There is much love, forgiveness, and understanding wrapped up in saying "I love you" to our children.

How much does a hug cost within the family?

To heal the heart is to forgive the family; I reach out with forgiveness and smile.

I do not need to see the person in my family whom I wish to forgive. I just feel it in my heart, and it is done.

I believe in myself completely; I must accept the family I was born into.

I search deep within to find faith in myself before I can find faith within my family.

My mother, father, brother, and sister are my blood. Can I help them? Can I forgive them?

I make a deliberate attempt to discipline myself daily not to judge my family but rather to forgive, love, and, if necessary, leave them.

Unconditional love is loving myself and my family from a distance, and completely letting go of the past to embrace the future.

What is my role within the family: to hurt, help, or heal?

❏ ✓ Checkmark page when learned/memorized

A working, nurturing, loving, forgiving, and understanding family is a true miracle.

I measure my worth by how I help heal the family.

What is a real family? A family that does not hide from the truth!

How important is love within the family? Do I need air to breathe?

Watch the children watching the mother showing the children how to love the father.

Watch the children watching the father showing the children how to love the mother.

Watch the children watching the parents showing the children how they themselves live.

Watch the children within the family learn how much love they have to work with as they prepare to leave the family.

Can I say I love the family that I was born into unconditionally? If I can, I am truly okay.

I can love my father and mother and forgive their behavior.

There is no pill, drink, or chemical that can give me the power to forget the family I came from.

The best medicine for forgiveness in the family is to sit still, stay quiet, and let myself feel within my heart.

Pride, ego, and arrogance destroy a family.

❏ ✔ Checkmark page when learned/memorized

How much does it really cost to always be right within my family?

Is there a family alive that can truly be bought?

Fantasize about the perfect family and search for a lifetime.

Anything or anyone that I cannot accept in my life, whatever I reject in my life, follows me around for the rest of my life!

What part of me are you? What do I need? What is my gift in life to give to you? What parts of me that are negative do I see in you?

Am I really "home" inside of me? Until I begin to develop the fact that I value all parts of myself—until I am aware of my "higher self"—until then, inside of me there remains no one home.

I recognize the "shadow" in my family and own it, embrace it, honor it. Without doing this, I create shadows in everything that I decide to disown.

Who is the scapegoat in my family? Who has become the caretaker of my family? Who has become the doormat in my family? Where are the caregivers in my family?

All the things in my past and in my family that I am afraid of are okay. All the sadness. It can bring awareness. All the darkness. It can bring light. All the fear. This can fade away.

Sometimes the child who lives within me feels that if I succeed in life I will never have a chance to be a child again.

❑ ✓ Checkmark page when learned/memorized

In families with abusive relationships: Take the fear and replace it with faith (love). Take the dark and let in the light (truth).

Take today and take a chance (trust). Today can be a new life. Tell the truth always.

Learn about the fears of the family. The past with your family, forgive them. Work on healing what is left over from the past in the family that you lived with.

To make me feel safe, I see myself surrounded in a warm light. I see my family surrounded in a warm light. I forgive anyone and everyone who has hurt me. I take a deep breath and go on to the next day.

A loving family has strong, democratic values; high expectations and goals for one another. Each family member loves, helps, respects, and forgives each other member. A healthy family has fun together and spends time together.

Going to school should not be the only source of happiness a child has. It should not be the only remaining means of providing children with hope. Children and parents should look forward to seeing each other at the end of the day.

Children must have hope within the family. Children need support in the family. Children need to feel they are loved in the family.

Toys, sports, new houses, clubs, vacations, and friends will never take the place of the parents just being there in the family and for the family.

❏✓ Checkmark page when learned/memorized

Once I lift someone to the level of laughing, they want to stay there. It feels good. I lift my awareness by smiling and try to learn to laugh at myself.

The constant busyness of the family, the constant running of the family, the constant sports loving of the family; when are they together quietly as a family?

In the family, if both husband and wife work all day and the children attend school all day and everyone is away all day, who takes the time to stop and say, "Let's take some time to be together today"?

A part of each day belongs to the family. A quiet time, a together time, a time to sit back at home together and really like it!

How can we appreciate one another in the family? Stop. Look at one another and ask, "What is on my mind?"

Mothers, talk to your daughters; fathers, listen to your sons; children, talk kindly to your parents; parents, hug your children.

Parents must learn to walk their talk and live by example. How else can a child be given an automatic okay to succeed in life?

Filter out the anger. Clean out the mind. Empty out the resentment. Let go of blame. I tell my spouse, child, brother, sister, or parent why I am upset today. I don't harbor resentments.

I find the reason why my family all came together. What have I got to learn from each of them? How can we help one another?

❏ ✓ Checkmark page when learned/memorized

The best doctors for the family are Dr. Eat-Right, Dr. Feel-Good, and Dr. Be-Still. They heal families worldwide.

I change my mind about the way I feel toward my family, and I change the family. My attitude is my choice.

If a family is divorced . . . forgive it. If a family is divided . . . support it. If a spouse is in darkness . . . mentally send that person light—lots and lots of light. See them encircled in white light.

Follow the yellow brick road to light and love in the family by being there for one another, even if the moment is temporarily inconvenient.

Just by asking each day for a hug, just by saying "I love you," just by saying "Don't worry, it's okay," just by saying "You are all right," just by being there—the family stays healed.

Families are all we have. Each person alive on this earth has roots. Each person picks a family for positive, definite lessons to learn.

Members within the family will listen to one another as well as they can hear one another.

A person within the family who holds on to bitterness sacrifices the future of the family staying together.

Once a person dies within the family, it is too late to admit you and he didn't see "eye to eye."

❏✓Checkmark page when learned/memorized

When a person within the family holds on to bitterness, the future of the family's togetherness becomes sacrificed.

Every person comes out of a family that was designed to teach him or her some very powerful lessons to learn about life.

Families have different reasons for coming together and different lessons to learn in falling apart.

How much time does each family member need to spend with every other member? Each needs to spend enough time to make a difference.

Every day I can give someone in my family a compliment, support, encouragement and love . . . especially lots of love.

People who make a commitment to one another, live together, support one another, trust in one another, and above all find time for one another are a focused and balanced family.

The father and the mother and the children all need to be friends. They need to laugh and play together and listen well.

Within the family are twenty-four golden hours. If eight to ten hours are for sleep and eight to ten hours are for work, this leaves four precious hours left in each day—for what?

Treasure the time that the children need. They are small for such a short while. Decide to learn from watching them grow.

When little things seem too big to carry, when everything seems to be closing in, remember to say, "Oh, normal day, let me be aware of the treasure you are."

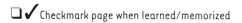 Checkmark page when learned/memorized

The family that spends time taking a walk together, praying together, listening together, eating together, laughing together . . . this is a strong, loving, loyal family.

Blended families exist to teach patience, understanding, and forgiveness. Whether we choose to learn the lesson is entirely up to us.

We each pick the family that we wish to be born into. This is a soul choice. There is no one to blame. A specific choice is made for specific growth.

The person in my family who presents the greatest challenge is usually the mirror of some great lesson that I am in the process of learning.

I fill my heart with understanding and try very hard to help my family grow by supporting them. I give them compassion and a big hug.

It is important to see the truth. The family member who hurts another has the ability to heal the heartache and forgive.

Families can live together in the light. If a family member sidesteps into darkness, let the person go. Let go and let God work.

Mothers and fathers are guardians of their children. Their children are on loan to them. Become friends with your children. Listen quietly to what they have to tell you about themselves.

❏ ✔ Checkmark page when learned/memorized

I cannot expect to have a lasting relationship with my children if I do not create lasting memories with them.

Children need to have examples they can follow in the family—namely, their parents.

I learn to parent my child by empathetically understanding the world of my child as my child perceives it.

Families who risk telling the truth discover more effective ways to achieve happiness, love, and peace within the family together. To risk loving is peaceful.

The key to success in the family is that respect plus communication equals forgiveness. Kids must have hope that their parents can get along together eventually.

I take time to talk to my children. I tell them the truth about how I feel. I tell them it is okay to make mistakes. They must learn from their mistakes. I give them examples of how they can make it better.

To have virtuous children we need to create a home life that will enhance the character and the mature part of the child—the kind that supports virtue.

With no regrets, one can say, "Before I die, I want to have raised healthy, happy, and strong children. I need to be optimistic internally."

❏ ✓ Checkmark page when learned/memorized

Chapter 4

FORGIVENESS

To forgive another person is to be free from guilt, denial, and fear.

❑ ✔ Checkmark page when learned/memorized

4th Ingredient: Forgiveness

"I believe forgiveness is suspending judgment on another."

There was so much work to do in healing myself once I realized I did not want to stay in the dark any longer. No matter what I did, how-ever, there always remained a feeling that something was missing. I took this feeling to mean I was lonely or I didn't have the support I needed. Constantly, I looked outside of myself for all of these answers.

What happened in a breath, took me years to grow toward. I first had to go through alcoholism, anxiety attacks, depression, illness, se-vere sadness, tremendous grief, and overwhelming hatred before I would ever consider there might be another option. It never dawned on me to consider forgiveness in any sense of the word.

I had done nothing wrong. I wasn't the one who had robbed my children of their grandmother! I wasn't the one who chose to kill my own mother for thirty-two dollars one hot morning in July! I wasn't the one who ruined everyone's life in an instant of horror and fury! Why should I ever forgive my brother for what he had done to our mother?

But a funny thing happens to a person when he or she goes through extreme trauma. The little everyday things in life that nor-mally bother you just don't matter anymore. Other issues that push people to a breaking point don't really have much significance either. Everything around you slows way down, and you start to look at the world with blinders off.

It's frightening at first to be so vulnerable. Yet for the first time in my life, I began to think with my heart and not my head. I had so many personal issues to be angry and mad about. I had gone through a divorce; I had become a workaholic; I had isolated myself from most of my friends. There was so much unresolved anger festering inside me.

Living my own life was like watching a movie being replayed. Over and over and over again, I wrestled with bitterness. I was almost able to anticipate the next hateful feeling before it appeared. I was becoming sick of it all, tired of being so obsessed with such hate and anger. It had been eating at me for a very long time.

One day I spoke at a convention, and afterward a man came up to me and asked to buy my book. We started talking, and he told me how much he agreed with my "recipe." This man also shed new light on how I looked at anger, hatred, and bitterness. He told me the story about the death of his only child. One night after coming home from a party, a drunk driver ran a stop sign and hit and killed his sixteen-year-old son, his only boy. He was a wonderful son, the man told me with a smile. The following day the two of them had planned to go on a canoe trip through the Canadian Boundary waters.

How could this man appear to be so genuinely happy? At one point, I watched him talking with someone else. He was actually smiling and interacting with others as though nothing this bad had ever happened in his lifetime. Then he said something that really made me stop and think.

"I believe in destiny," he said, smiling. "I believe when it was my son's time to leave this earth, nothing anyone could have done would have stopped this. It was my son's time to go. I'm so fortunate I had the time with him that I did."

I thought a lot about what this man said to me. I started to realize that his belief system and how he viewed his own life kept him from passing judgment and enabled him to forgive readily. He explained to me that forgiveness has a lot to do with personality, ego, and pride. I asked him, "How did you let go of ill feelings, bad attitudes, and hatreds you could have adopted throughout your whole lifetime?"

"In a breath," he said. "Just tell yourself it doesn't matter anymore. Your past is like going to the movies and watching old tapes. Everything that has happened to you in the past is gone. The only part that keeps it connected to you is the emotion. *This is what matters most to you. All you would have to do is quit thinking about something that is pressing on you and replace it with a nice thought. Or try to see yourself with a week remaining to live. What are your priorities now in life? Do you still harbor a grudge, and do hatreds still abound? Try forgiveness on the way you would try on a new pair of shoes . . . do it slowly and see what happens."*

I realized my harbored resentments and hatred were what kept the fires of hatred burning. I was entitled to my anger, after all. What else did I have left when my brother had robbed me of my mother and all I cherished about her? I summarized my thoughts and brought this to his attention.

He smiled and spoke. "Each person has lessons to learn from, and from these lessons choices occur. It is a choice to go forward and grow. It is a choice to forgive and forget. It is a choice to decide not to judge another person's behavior but to move on instead." Such warm beautiful eyes this man had. I remember my grandma telling me, "The eyes are the window to the soul. Kind eyes, kind heart."

What would be wrong with my trying to clear my slate? I had tried everything else and nothing else had worked. Nothing outside of myself healed me inside. I would try for the first time to say silently, "I forgive others who have hurt me." I would try this on . . . I would see how that felt.

The first couple of weeks went slowly. I continued to revert to old ways, dredging up old memories of hurt feelings and terrible remorse. Still, I was determined to continue. "I forgive others for hurting me," I continued to tell myself. One night before going to bed, I felt a feeling of relief and release all at the same time. It was as if I were watching myself from outside of myself. A tremendous load lifted from my shoulders, and I felt free. I smiled to myself and remembered what the man had told me: "It will come in a breath."

Key to Ingredient 4: When I forgive, I regain my own inner strength.

Forgiveness in life is as important as life itself.

When we are able to let go of anger and forgive, we can move very quickly to where we were supposed to be going from the start.

When I learn forgiveness, I know that I am automatically forgiven, unconditionally.

The burden can be lifted from the heavy heart. When I reach out to forgive what is in my past, I can then live in the "now."

To forgive another human being is to be free from all guilt, denial, and fear. Let go of ego.

❏ ✓ Checkmark page when learned/memorized

What is fear? *F*alse *E*vents *A*ppearing *R*eal.

To be able to forgive, a person must be able to let go of five thoughts. I let go of anger, greed, guilt, denial, and all my fear right now.

Nothing that happens to me ever happens by mistake. There are no mistakes, only lessons for me to learn from. I am learning my lessons.

First, we must be able to look at ourselves, forgive ourselves for any type of anger, judgment, and resentment; and then forgive everyone else whom we blame, dislike, and/or resent.

It does a person no good to carry burdens from the past. It is old, stinky, rotten garbage. It weighs down the human heart with disease, discomfort, and pain. *To forgive others, I heal myself, and eventually others heal from my example.*

When we forgive, we learn to see others in the light, not in the darkness. All thoughts come back to where they originally began.

Feeling forgiveness allows the soul to sit quietly back and feel safety.

Let go of gossip and feel the judgment release.

Who can judge another soul without feeling the pains and pulse of one's own shortcomings?

❏ ✓ Checkmark page when learned/memorized

The reasons we feel forgiveness are the reasons we have for living. Each and every day we are given the reason to be forgiven.

To feel forgiveness for another human being allows us opportunity to right ourselves with God.

Greatness starts not by achieving material wealth, but the real wealth we acquire will be from the forgiveness we give to another.

I start each day with a clean slate. I forgive myself for everything, and I forgive everyone for anything they have done that has hurt me. I am beginning to see life from my "higher self."

Far from the road to recovery we stray when we insist on carrying anger, resentment, and remorse in our hearts. I can learn to forgive others unconditionally.

To go that extra little mile and forgive is to grow a lifetime in a moment.

Never has so much been sacrificed for so little without forgiveness.

I free my heart, my health, and all my happiness by forgiving this moment everything and everyone that has ever hurt me in any way.

It is in the giving of love that I let down my guard of anger and open doors to forgiveness. I find fulfillment and freedom from all my fears.

❑ ✓ Checkmark page when learned/memorized

Finding the place in my mind that I can go to quietly, I ask for the help that I need to forgive. I know that unless I do this, I cannot find total peace.

I fear nothing by forgiving everyone who has hurt me. I can now achieve everything that is needed for my own personal higher growth in this lifetime.

Reaching out to another person for help, I ask for the guidance to learn to forgive. I will try this today.

I take a moment to step away from my personality, and I see the forgiveness of a higher self that is really me. I love myself for who I am.

A person who desires to have peace must reason with the heart, not the mind, bringing forgiveness into view.

To please all within and all without is to know the comfort in a forgiving family.

What can you find to really give? Just *forgive.*

Deep inside we find what we search for is not in the mind, but in the heart. Forgiveness lies buried deep within our heart.

There is no person who can know the trials and tribulations of another. How can we possibly carry any judgments of others? We can only forgive. In forgiving, we grow beyond our wildest dreams.

❏ ✓ Checkmark page when learned/memorized

When people want to leave this world, they are insecure. They need lots of hugs, kisses, and love. They do not need judgment. I can say I love you.

By forgiving, I realize a happy experience. Therefore, I become a happy person. I can focus on peace and harmony. I can let go of all hurt.

"I'm sorry," "Forgive me," and "I love you" are the three keys to fulfilling relationships and three statements that are so often missing.

Without forgiveness, the person cannot be whole. The body is the instrument of the soul. Think of it this way: if a piano player were to get sick, would it help things to fix the piano?

When I forgive, I love unconditionally and I will regain the power that I have temporarily lost. I know that love heals my personality. Underneath every crisis of hatred and anger is a decision to use my highest power.

In order to move forward in life I must be able to look honestly at myself with courage and remove the defenses, saying, "I can forgive myself."

The way to forgiveness lies in being able to look clearly at all the places in my life. If I feel I have lost my power where others have controlled me, I forgive and take back my power.

When I forgive others, I come to the awareness that they are always going to have to be responsible for their own life and what they have done. I, however, release any dark thoughts I have about others. I forgive others if they have hurt me.

The more I desire to heal myself, the stronger the desire will be to forgive others unconditionally. I can now go forward with my journey in life and close the doors to all pain and hurt and anger.

I challenge myself today and ask: "How would it hurt me if I forgave that person one hundred percent, unconditionally?" I can tell them so . . . or send them a letter or just see them surrounded in God's love and light. I can move on.

To forgive is to grow in the knowing that I also will be forgiven. To see people who hurt me surrounded in light brings their life in focus. When I send them light, I send them truth as it is, not as they know it. They start to change.

When I release anger and become forgiving, my awareness suddenly shifts into a forward and upward motion and into the higher frequencies of light and love.

Unforgiveness does not work. When I realize that the journey in life has to do with becoming whole, I will see that situations are presented to each of us as lessons to learn from daily.

If it is true that all people will eventually evolve into wholeness and empowerment with light and love, then why wait? I can forgive others today. Everything on earth evolves eventually. Which way am I choosing to evolve today? Am I learning?

There is a great and mystifying power in forgiveness, a cleansing

❏ ✓ Checkmark page when learned/memorized

that allows the soul to breathe and live in light with freedom from negativity and darkness.

To forgive transcends the earthly way of thinking in dark thoughts and despair. By taking the other person's fears on, truly trying to walk down another's path and considering that person's position, I can learn to heal at an impersonal level. I remove the emotion from it.

Forgiveness is truly and completely a healing within the heart, a knowing that it will be okay to let go of one's ego, pride, and hurt, and I will be a better and different person.

Every time I decide to make a choice for my higher self (to forgive), I align myself with light and I give myself great personal power.

It is of the utmost importance to be brave and courageous, to feel the strains of the heart asking to forgive the other person, to let go of pride and arrogance, and to just forgive.

If I can bring myself to forgive myself and others for all faults and misgivings and say, "There but for the grace of God go I," I am a powerful soul empowered in light and love. I go forth with no regrets.

❏ ✓ Checkmark page when learned/memorized

Chapter 5

DISCIPLINE

How powerful can I be if I never doubt myself again?

❑ ✓ Checkmark page when learned/memorized

5th Ingredient: Discipline

*"I discipline myself to find my personal power,
refusing to doubt myself again."*

*Throughout my life, I fought hard to stay positive and not give in to
fear. I never put a label on it, but I knew from my successes that I
had discipline. Still, no matter how much I prepared each day, I was
unprepared for the brutal way in which my mother died. Her murder robbed me of my own personal power, which I had built up over
the years.*

*One of the hardest things for me to do was to try not to think
about how my mother had died. After her murder, my thoughts
would keep going back to the scene where it had happened—her
house. Over and over again, my mind would silently video each and
every room in which she had lived. Everything that had happened
that terrible morning had left horrifying pictures engraved deep
within my mind. I simply could not stop thinking about that day. I
stopped being the top producer I had become at work. My self-
confidence and courage quickly evaporated. I was overcome with
sadness, depression, and all-consuming fear.*

*All my energy was lost. I had little discipline, and my personal
power was gone. How could I bring myself to think good thoughts
again?*

*Most of us think more than fifty thousand thoughts a day. Usu-
ally, they are the same thoughts as the day before. Everything around
us was at some prior time a thought. This puts us in an extraordi-*

nary place. In order to benefit from our thoughts, we must first believe we have personal power. Then we must try hard to use our power in positive, beneficial ways.

Everything that has happened to us in life shapes our world. Anything negative affects the quality of the life we live. It isn't so much the events themselves but what we think of them that affects us. Most important of all, it is the feelings behind the thoughts we think that give rise to our power. My grandma used to say to me, "Keep worrying about something that hasn't happened and eventually it will." Our thoughts give seed to weeds or flowers. When we change our thinking in a positive way, we become healthy.

My life had to change.

I began to read as much as I could about depression. There were new holistic avenues to pursue, health and nutritional areas to research. As many books as I read, the same information kept reappearing: "Find the higher power within yourself and you will find peace."

I had been searching for that peace everywhere but inside me. The more I kept reading, the more I had to admit that a belief in God gave me a feeling of peace. That belief brought an immediate, bottomless source of peace to me.

Still, at times, dark pictures reappeared. I was stuck in a place I could not leave. Just a few short months earlier, I had been able to do ten to twenty different things in a day. I prided myself in accomplishing so much. I was able to handle any problem with little difficulty, jump any hurdle. Now a simple trip to the mailbox took exhausting effort.

At last, in my search for truth and after all the reading I had done, I came across a simple example of visualization that took on a new meaning for me. I disciplined my mind to think about something wonderful. I visualized a beautiful beach in Florida with miles of white sand. I saw myself sitting in the middle of this beach, in my very own sandbox with huge buckets of sand around me. Everyone I know comes to me and fills his or her bucket, until my own sandbox is completely empty. With my supply exhausted, I reach outside the sandbox to an unlimited supply of sand around me on the beach. Even if someone took all my sand from me, I could still step out onto the beach and refill my sandbox with this unlimited supply.

Finally, I could relate to the sand in the sandbox as being my own personal power and the source feeding my power as coming from an unlimited supply in the universal mind of God.

In my visualization, I see and hear ocean waves. They bring as much water as I need to make anything I want in the sand. I can build a beautiful house, a lovely garden, a swimming pool. I make myself think about this beautiful beach every time dark thoughts start to creep into my mind.

This part takes discipline.

The mind records every piece of information it takes in. Everything we see and hear is stored there. I must retrain and discipline *my mind to think new, beautiful thoughts. No other way can I avoid rethinking the same thoughts.*

Someone taking my sand away from me is a symbol of others trying to rob me of my own personal power. The more good things I visualize in my mind, the more good things come into my life. When I get angry, fearful, and sad, I drain away my personal power. If I revert to negative thoughts that deplete this positive power, I am on my own. I know where that has taken me, down a dead-end street lined with pride and ego. I now know how to leave the fear-based life and live a life filled with discipline.

It can be as simple as looking at the glass half full, or half empty.

All good comes to me when I quiet myself and ask for inner direction.

Key to Ingredient 5: I discipline myself to find my own personal power.

Life without discipline is an empty shell of existence based on nothingness, drifting back and forth amidst a storm of discontent.

To have discipline is to help oneself. To recognize weakness is to love oneself. To apply discipline daily is to give oneself the utmost respect.

Why have discipline? Because it is a major key to peace, tranquillity, and completeness.

Discipline in everyday life begins with the moment, then comes the hour, and eventually the day and the week. Soon months and years have discipline behind them.

I design my life with discipline in my behavior, in my thinking, and in my eating. I am on the road to success at all times.

To know the importance of discipline in my life, I look at my life as I would look at going on a trip somewhere I have never been. I would always take a map with me.

Disciplining my life, I decide to try to live life a little better, far more honest, and a lot more structured each day.

How can we discipline our children if we ourselves are not disciplined?

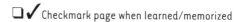 Checkmark page when learned/memorized

It starts with saying, "I'm okay. I can start today. I can discipline myself to do the things that are right for me to grow today."

I believe I have a lower self and a higher self. Discipline keeps me in balance and focused on my higher self.

Without discipline we deny our true identity.

We are on track when we have discipline in our daily life. We know what we should and can't do. We can set boundaries for ourselves. We base these boundaries on our principles, not on what others say.

Discipline decides my day. Weakness wastes it away. *I am a disciplined person today.*

Every person has worth. It is up to each person to find his or her worth and thereby realize a purpose for being.

Discipline guides the way each day.

Discipline directs; to give in, neglects.

Change the present problem by disciplining the self to do what has to be done for the highest and best concern of self.

I truly love myself as much as I am able to discipline myself to do whatever my higher self tells me to do.

There is a wall called discipline that is erected between the higher self and the lower self.

❑ ✓ Checkmark page when learned/memorized

A day, a week, a month must have discipline. At the end of the year it's time to "close doors."

I try very hard not to control another person's life. I control my own life with discipline.

Discipline carries the tools of self-respect, honesty, and love for oneself and others.

The darkness of the day shifts to the light and brings discipline into my life and direction for where it is that I need to be going. I am safe.

Sometimes life seems to overpower me with anger from the past, demands of the present, and false hopes for tomorrow. Still, I dare to discipline my day and keep moving forward.

Discipline rewards us with gratitude, gratefulness, and no regrets for yesterday gone by.

One way for me to get on top of my problems is to understand that disciplining my day brings understanding and love for myself.

Discipline decides and contributes to the true character of a human being.

Without balance—doing the right amount of everything each day—discipline is pointless.

I go deep within myself and I ask for discipline, direction, and discernment . . . daily.

❏✔ Checkmark page when learned/memorized

Beautiful qualities arise in one when one is able to discipline one's life with humility, love, and understanding. It is then that one is able to achieve and find forgiveness.

We create all of our problems. They do not disappear until we clear our conscience.

If I dwell on what I do not have, I put energy into it. Whatever I put my thoughts on grows. The more I notice what I am thankful for, and what I have, the more I will receive from the universe.

By disciplining ourselves to forgive others, we quit judging them. We release the past and go on to the future.

Life cannot work perfectly unless we discipline ourselves to have harmonious relationships. We seek people who are basically like ourselves.

To release discomfort inside oneself, one must release unloving thoughts about another human being.

I learn to pay attention to things in life. I look hard and learn so much more. Every day it is important to learn something new.

Design your life with discipline to start the day. Drink two large glasses of purified water. I eat bran in the morning and some fruit and herbal tea.

I start my day with discipline. First thing every morning I find quiet time, if only five or ten minutes. I sit quietly and reflect on my breathing. Slow, deep breaths. I breathe in through my nose and out through my mouth.

❑ ✔ Checkmark page when learned/memorized

I discipline my thoughts by beginning my day with only positive thoughts in my mind. I carefully remove all other thoughts from my mind.

I discipline myself to focus on as many positive affirmations as I can think of at that moment. Example: "I am aware. I am bright. I am calm. I am disciplined. I am enlightened. . . ."

Discipline takes memorization. The mind needs to rethink what it thinks about. What we put into the mind stays there until we replace it with different thinking.

Discipline means I start out each day with a good feeling about myself. It is important to love myself and forgive myself and discipline myself.

Discipline the body, and the mind will grow. Discipline the mind, and the heart will heal. When the heart heals, the hurt is removed. With the hurt gone, hope is everywhere.

When a person is really hurting and grieving and feeling sadness that appears to be overwhelming, it is best to discipline oneself to learn something new. Learning is growing. Growing is healing. Healing is discipline in action.

Throughout my day, wherever I am, I practice thinking positive affirmations, especially in my car while I am driving. I also listen to positive awareness tapes.

I discipline myself to eat only good food. I know that what I eat affects how I feel and how I think. I try hard to discipline myself to stay away from sweets, soft drinks, and chemicals.

❏ ✔ Checkmark page when learned/memorized

Discipline during the day is crucial. I have only today. Yesterday is not mine anymore, and tomorrow is not yet here. Today I can concentrate on doing what is best for my body.

Today I will concentrate on disciplining myself to have one half hour of exercise. I will also go for a long walk outside and appreciate nature and what it is showing me.

Today I will discipline myself to quiet my thoughts more and focus on feeling good. I feel good, and I feel happy. I am content and at peace with myself and everyone else.

Discipline involves purposely wanting to remove old thought patterns and habits that do not fit. Deciding to concentrate and focus on forgiveness. Forgiving myself for anything and everything that has been done to me. Disciplining my heart to heal with forgiving myself first of all.

Each and every day is new. A brand new day to start a brand new way. Discipline that decides each day helps a person to focus on growing, healing, and happiness always.

Today—all day—I will discipline myself to remove all negative thinking from my mind. I will think only positive thoughts about other people.

I position myself to expect change instantly when I am able to allow myself to start my day with discipline. All day long, I remember that I am in charge of my destiny.

❏ ✔ Checkmark page when learned/memorized

Chapter 6

WORK

*Every soul comes to earth
with a specific mission.*

☐ ✓ Checkmark page when learned/memorized

6th Ingredient: Work

"I believe every soul comes to earth for a specific purpose."

One day I was doing a book signing for Barnes & Noble, and a very distinguished older man walked up to me out of the crowd. He told me he had been a CEO of a large company for over thirty years, yet he was unprepared for what life dealt him when his twenty-six-year-old son committed suicide. He said his life went into a tailspin, and he poured himself into his work. No matter how long the hours he worked, nothing could bring him relief. One day someone handed him my book, and he said his life changed for the better overnight. He just wanted to thank me.

What is our true purpose in life? To find fulfillment, self-worth, and self-respect. Work is truly the way to find self-esteem. If a person has good health and a social security number and is of age, he or she is capable of some kind of work. It is important to ask yourself, What exactly is the value of my life? How can I contribute to my own happiness, my own peace of mind, and achieve good health every day?

By doing what comes naturally. Each of us has natural talents.

The universe has given each of us a biological time clock. The universe prepares us and often gives us painful lessons to learn by. Perhaps you've been let go from a job. Perhaps there is a death or divorce in your family. Perhaps a relationship is challenging. Perhaps you have a serious illness to contend with. All of these lessons are opportunities for change and internal growth. Are we ready for a new mission? Will we decide to take it? We are being asked to institute change in our daily life. It is up to each of us to go forward. Complications arise out of fear—fear of the unknown, fear of going forward, fear of closing doors to an old job.

Too often, we remain stuck in a comfortable position that becomes all too familiar. Some people remain at a job for ten to twenty years solely out of habit. This mindset builds a box in which we live day to day, and gradually, little by little, we see only what is inside of the box. A job that may at one time have been temporary becomes lifelong. A work position that once may have been a stepping-stone becomes a boulder.

I was a professional businessperson dedicated to my job. Then one day tragedy hit and I hid behind my work. I became a workaholic night and day. My family and personal friendships all moved to a back burner.

When we come to the end of the road, when life is over and done, when we are alive no more, will we wish we had worked longer at a job? If your life ended today, do you feel in your heart your days were spent trying hard to accomplish a mission on earth that engrossed all your highest creative talents and made you happy? The clock is ticking. . . .

In my darkness and despair, I found a new talent I was ready for.

You might be reading this now and saying to yourself, "Yes, it's easy for her to say, just quit my job, go find something brand-new to do, just satisfy my heart's content. Who will pay the bills, how will money come in, where will the next paycheck come from?"

A new way of thinking has to set in. Remember the old saying "Keep doing the same things, and be assured, the same things will happen."

How many people take a vacation or venture into a new place without obtaining a map to first guide them where to go? Yet every day we dive headfirst into new jobs without investigating the pros and cons first.

How many years have you given yourself to a job not totally fulfilling? Do you go to work day in and day out feeling empty and lifeless? As good as I was at selling homes, I did not feel fulfilled at what I did.

Ask yourself now, "Who am I? What have I come here to accomplish?"

In the morning when I wake up and in the evening before retiring, this is when I take time for me. I begin silently questioning my true purpose here.

Find a quiet spot, sit still, and close your eyes.
Ask yourself, what do I want in my life?
What price am I willing to pay to get this?
How can I go about changing my life?

Put your hands together and ask for guidance on this. Answers will come.

If you simply start with this, you are miles ahead of yourself already. When you finish reading, take a blank sheet of paper. Make a wish list of all the "wants" you would bring into your life if this were possible. Try not to give in to fear. Your lower self may be saying you will fail if you do this, so why even try? Yet if you even write down one thing on this wish list, you are already successful. Awareness comes slowly. One small step at a time. Don't look too far down the road.

Tomorrow is a new day.

I was in real estate for twenty-six years. Often I would give talks to my fellow agents on the merits of selling. People would say, "You should write a book. Real estate agents need a field manual." I thought this was a silly suggestion. "How could I write a book?" My life was in sales. Yet I continued to feel empty inside. There remained an unfulfilled place inside of me I could not fix. Then I started to meditate and pray on a daily basis for at least a half hour. I found the time I took for myself brought me to a new understanding and awareness of "who" I really was. In my busy day, I eliminated much television and talking aimlessly on the telephone to other people about their daily problems. I began to dedicate one hour a day just to myself. This one hour turned into page after page of a real estate manual that came to life over six years ago. I sold my book, Inside Story of Real Estate Manual, *to a publisher and my life took on a new dimension. One day at a time, I began to integrate new routines that were positive in my life. I meditated, ate well, kept a journal, worked out, and met new people. I became aware of how multitalented I was.*

Key to Ingredient 6: I ask for guidance to find my highest purpose of work.

What is the true purpose of work? To find fulfillment, self-worth, and self-respect.

Work is the only antidote for boredom.

If I have my health and a social security number and am of age, I am capable of contributing my talents through some kind of work.

❑ ✓ Checkmark page when learned/memorized

What is the value of my life? To be able to work with the talents that I am given. What are they?

Every person has the potential to work at what he or she is good at. We all have talents.

There are many parts of a person and many different jobs a person is capable of handling at one time. I know I can do many good things.

Parents need to realize that balance is important. Give equal time to work and children.

Teaching children the importance of working begins at a very early age around the house.

Work is the foundation for merit and goal setting throughout a person's life. What is a workaholic? A person who feels that his or her *first* priority is work.

How can a person who desperately needs money, must work constantly, and has children that are continually taking a backseat find balance? By going within to find a way out.

I work hard to find the way in which I am meant to truly serve.

Throughout my life there will always be possibilities through different kinds of work. No job is too menial or insignificant for me.

I watch the opportunities that are given to me. When I think I have lost a job, I may be able to find myself for the first time.

❏ ✓ Checkmark page when learned/memorized

How can I find the real reasons I am put on this earth? What should I work at? I am still; I ask myself; then I wait and listen.

To be successful at my work I must manage my time and be disciplined.

Do it now! (The toughest part.)

What is more important to get behind me and/or put in front of me? I stay with one thing at a time until it is finished.

I am aware that if I risk doing what I must do, my life will become balanced in spite of my fears.

To find my sense of purpose I ask, "What do I want? What price will I pay to get it?"

I learn to be excellent at what I can do. Contribute. Be creative. Be responsible. Make an effort. Stay with it. I memorize these.

Stress is doing less than I can with my higher self. I enjoy my life.

What do I want to do? Do I know? Do I have a "want list" for my life? What will comfort me? What keeps up my interest? What keeps me enthusiastic? What am I committed to now and for the rest of my life? I can have anything I want, but most people don't *know* what they want.

One should discuss and work on problems with an attitude that fully intends to solve them.

❏ ✓ Checkmark page when learned/memorized

Once I succeed in business, I can go on to other things I like. There is an unlimited supply of opportunities in the universe for me.

I must decide what I want. I sit quietly and surround myself in light. I ask for direction and write it down. I am learning.

If I don't like what I am doing enough to be better or the best at it, it is not right for me.

I accept one hundred percent of the responsibility for my own life. If I make excuses, I am going backward. I will turn around.

I must have courage to go for it. Better still is to stay with it. I am not afraid.

One must not be afraid to step out of old patterns and ways. I can become stronger than I thought I could be by taking a risk, taking a new position, taking on the light of a new awareness and going forward.

In the dark moments of uncertainty (when the whole world looks futile, one can't go forward or backward, and life is in a state of flux), I must be brave, for I am capable of far more than I think I am.

I am capable of becoming smarter, faster, and better at achieving more of my goals than I ever dreamed of doing simply by focusing my thoughts on something new about myself and believing I have a purpose.

❏✔ Checkmark page when learned/memorized

There is a creative solution to every problem. Every person has the power to think in new directions and change his or her current situation if it is negative.

If I am constantly working to improve myself and the things that I do each day, then everything that happens to me happens for a reason and purpose. In my work I go forward or backward by choice.

What is missing in my work? Can my talents be put to use in a better way? Am I gifted in some other direction that I am more suited to and better qualified for? What is the reason for the wait? Setbacks are never an enemy but rather a "hidden friend."

By becoming inner-focused and learning to go within, we become aware of our hidden talents and inner resources. We are calling upon our higher self to show us our real gifts and talents.

I ask daily for help from a higher power to give direction for purpose. I am protected.

Dig deep within yourself. Watch your emotions and your mind. Don't give in to panic and negativity. I listen quietly within for the guidance and understanding of what I am truly supposed to be working on in this lifetime.

I tell myself that I am unstoppable. No person, thing, or event can stop me from achieving a goal for myself in this lifetime (if the goal is for my highest good).

❏ ✓ Checkmark page when learned/memorized

As I go through life, there will be many people, encounters, and messages given to me. These are to show me the path I am to take.

The soul came to earth to work hard. Each person has a job that is specific. There are many other things a person is qualified for, but one "true purpose" that brings inner peace.

If the job I am in is unfulfilling, I look all around me. I search within me. I look outside of my normal scope of vision and feel the true mission I am to take.

It does not matter what I am doing, I can do more. It matters not what the past has dealt me, I can try harder. All that counts is when I let go. Trust, and move on!

Work should be challenging, exciting, and fulfilling. If it is not, I am not challenging, exciting, and fulfilling myself!

I never regret what I have not done. I do not feel my current job is a mistake. I take today and find a way. I realize my divine, higher self-purpose and ask the universe, "What is my current job teaching me?"

One can only enjoy life when one enjoys all parts of one's life. I can only appreciate life when I look deep within and find my true purpose for work while on this planet.

There is a stigma attached to society that says one job is sufficient. Each person is capable of multidimensional tasks. Each

❑ ✓ Checkmark page when learned/memorized

soul comes to earth totally equipped for what he or she has chosen to do.

When we find what challenges us the most, when we know that we have a mission to do, we realize that true peace lies within.

Each soul work becomes a "perfect project." Work leads each person up the ladder of life. The ladder of life is a masquerade of different challenges, lessons, and encounters. It is up to us to keep going.

Work is never done. Our mission is ongoing. Each of us has an obligation to the other to help, heal, and personally contribute to the world.

Perhaps work would and should and will be summed up in the following truth principle. Work: "To be able to realize one's true mission on earth and accomplish daily what one's higher self set out to do before coming here."

Chapter 7

MONEY

*Being rich means leading
a balanced life.*

7th Ingredient: Money

"I measure my true worth not by the amount of money I have."

Every single day we deal with extreme issues involving charge account excess, budget plans, money problems, and stress. Daily we look for a one-way trip out of debt. For many, this does nothing more than accentuate the desire for material security. Everything we say we need revolves around money. Money has become our security blanket, and "purchasing power" has replaced "people caring."

I remember being at a bookstore, signing copies of an earlier edition of this book. A woman walked up to me and said, "Why should I pay money for that book when I don't see any credentials by your name for writing it? What makes you an authority on life?" I told her to turn to the front pages and read the introduction to the book. She disappeared for a while, and pretty soon she came back to the table where I was sitting. "I'll take six books, please," she said. There was a tear in the corner of her eye. She realized we are all experts on life and we are here to teach one another.

How is it possible to lead a balanced life amid problems of divorce, turmoil, job loss, and continuous debt? By taking one day at a time, one lesson to learn from at a time. I was going through my mail and recalled a particular letter that really touched me.

Janine (not her real name) was married and had two children. For more than ten years, the couple appeared to be living a comfortable lifestyle. Janine had a part-time job. Her husband, for the most part, supported the family. Outside, all seemed normal. Inside, it was a different story. After years of silent treatment and friction, the husband had become bitter and angry. Constant work, money problems, and family turmoil had turned his wife moody and distant.

On Valium for two years, she felt that nothing really helped. The children were teenagers now and lived in a world of their own. A son, seventeen, was intelligent but quick-tempered and reclusive. He had few friends. His parents were going to be glad to see him graduate, hoping problems at school would end. Their daughter was sixteen. At one point, she had curly blond hair and good grades. Now, with short black hair, she and her boyfriend dressed in dark clothing, listened to heavy rock music, and tattooed various body parts. The parents were at a loss for what to do. They couldn't even solve their own problems.

What does money have to do with all of this?

Over the years, the family had eaten meals at fast-food places, lived at sporting events, raced through each day, and gone to bed at night dog-tired. Loud music and television blared twenty-four hours a day. There was no quiet in this house, and everyone lived together—separately. Sundays were for catching up with chores and errands. God was not spoken of and spirituality had not been introduced. A feeling of anger permeated the air. The husband worked at a job he didn't necessarily enjoy but that paid well. Lack of joy blocked creative juices in the entire family.

At dinner one evening, the husband announced he was "doing his own thing." He'd always wanted to go to Hawaii; he was leaving in two weeks. First, however, he was moving his things out of the house and in with his secretary, who was going to Hawaii with him. He was filing for divorce immediately. The wife began to cry in disbelief. Both children stared at the wall and said nothing.

A year went by and the divorce had become messy. The husband lived with his secretary full-time and had not seen his children in months. The wife lived at home with rooms bare of furniture. A prescription of Prozac, along with sedatives, was by her side. Her entire world, night and day, focused on what her husband had done to her. She told everyone she saw.

She worried about money.

The source of income from her husband dried up considerably. Left alone on a small monthly income she was told to budget everything, write it down, and give it to the attorney. Her attorney suggested she moved into an apartment and get a real job. Filled with contempt, anger, and fear, she had no more money for the attorney and felt her husband owed her plenty. Where would money come from if she was forced out of the house?

This scenario plagues a large percentage of households today. What could Janine have done about her money problems? How could she have eliminated worry and balanced her life with everything around her pulling her down? First, she said, she began by reading my book. She then decided to accept a concept. "Everything happens to each of us for a reason." A very powerful lesson was waiting to be learned.

Janine read my book and slowly her life began to take on a new meaning. She wound up getting a small loan, going back to school, and becoming a nurse. This was something she had dreamed of doing as a teen and had put away in the back of her mind.

Is this lesson really about money?

When a person is given severe tests, especially involving money, it is easy to get sidetracked. What would I do in a situation like this? The first thing I would do is give up all chemicals in my system. I favor holistic healing. Next, I would sit down with both my children and tell them how much I love them, for they are not at fault. I would not speak ill of their father. Again—I would not speak ill of their father.

I would tell them we would find a way to get through this together and hope we could all work on forgiveness. I would find a way to exercise my body and my mind each day for at least a half hour and invite the children to do the same. I would find a good spiritual counselor who would give me appointments and charge me on a graduated scale according to what I could pay. I would find a religious organization that I felt comfortable with and encourage my children to go with me. I would buy a copy of Louise Hay's book You Can Heal Your Life. *She explains why illness comes.*

I would give my house a good cleaning and have a garage sale. Junk food gone, I would start to eat healthy food. I would contact a financial consultant and try to consolidate my own debt. With prayer, I would quietly start looking at new options.

Is this really a blessing in disguise?

Everything seems to revolve around money, but does it really? As sad as this family is right now, there is opportunity to start new. Money is only one measure of self-worth for those not able to sit quietly and go within. It is impossible to heal a wounded heart just by making money. One must find the hurt, listen to the heart, and start again. Now the real person can be found.

Starting over with balance in all areas of life allows old wounds to heal. When you integrate forgiveness, miracles begin to happen. There will never be enough money in the world to bring us happiness if all we look for is financial security. When all is lost around me, I pray, believe, and trust that I am protected. If I have no job, no husband, and no friends, I must seek spiritual help. This takes courage. I believe this is not the end, only a test.

Money will always be in the background, waiting to be claimed. In the stillness of my heart I can hear my higher self give direction for moving forward—and money will come.

> **Key to Ingredient 7: When I find my true talent, the money will come.**

Money is the motivation for one to realize one's potential, worth, and ambitions from a materialistic point of view.

Money is a teacher in life.

The value of money is often never learned in one lifetime.

Money always brings to those who "want" complete temporary satisfaction.

Money truly is a source of possessing power and having the ability to choose.

As we go through life, we must learn why we need money in the amounts we feel we do.

Ambition, drive, and substance: how much do they have to do with the amounts of money we bring into our lives over the years?

Money manages to keep people together for the most superficial reasons.

❏✓ Checkmark page when learned/memorized

A person can grow old in a few short years by replacing the most important values with the almighty dollar.

It is important to make money. It is more important to know what I want for myself internally before I focus on the external needs in my life.

When I realize my worth, money becomes second nature to my more evolved value system.

Money can be a magic cure for many wants, needs, and frustrations. It also can be a Band-Aid that covers the cancer.

Start quickly and quietly finding out why money is important to you at the level it is.

If I have no money, I am fortunate in being able to start at the beginning.

A cynical person may say, "It's easy for you to say. You don't pay my bills." But what have I got going for myself after I pay the bills?

More money is needed as I shut my eyes to situations around me.

Money manifests anger, resentment, and greed quicker than flies take to honey.

I can make myself feel happy by making just the right amount of money.

❑ ✔ Checkmark page when learned/memorized

Mend a quarrel, forgetting the long-overdue debt.

I measure my worth not by the amount of money I have, but rather by asking, If I should lose all my money today, how much am I truly worth?

I minimize the amount owed to me. Rather, I maximize the service that I have given.

Goals are something magical. They have the ability to teach me how to visualize and create the amount of abundance that is mine.

A person, job, and money must all be looked at carefully.

I let go of why, when, and where I was not given what I deserve. I begin today to believe that now I can, will, and shall have whatever is meant to come to me.

If it is for my highest good and the highest good of all concerned, the right amounts of money always will come my way. I work hard.

I treasure my self-worth above my monetary worth at any and all times.

When I create external goals that require monetary gain, I learn to identify the tests that are given to me along the way.

Money never satisfies the internal goals of my higher-self value system. Money is only the frosting on the cake.

❏ ✓ Checkmark page when learned/memorized

Do I need what I want to buy with the money that I have? Or do I buy things out of boredom?

I measure the amounts of money that come into my life with the sifter of understanding, forgiveness, and acceptance that will help me grow into my own powerful potential.

Money always has two distinct, different, and diabolical faces. It challenges and changes us.

The level that I am at requires the amount of money that I need for where I am at *now!*

There is an illusion that surrounds money. What is it? How much of my time do I spend acquiring or requiring for myself?

The universe truly has an abundant supply of money for every man, woman, and child if they believe, visualize, and accept.

Children are to be taught the value that comes from learning that money is a tool for facilitating the need.

Money is the only measure of self-worth for those who are not able to go within.

Money has the distinction of keeping parents distanced from their children too much of the time. The parents become workaholics.

How much money is enough to replace the years lost working while my children grew up?

❑ ✓ Checkmark page when learned/memorized

To measure the right amount of money I need, I use the yard-stick of love, and I am always fair with myself.

I distance myself from those who seek me only for material worth and not my real worth.

A person's friends come not from the amounts of money he or she makes, but rather from the ability to give from the heart and not judge.

Must we make so much money, or so little, that life becomes worthless?

People who do not know their inner worth feel their "true worth" is determined by their outer worth.

How can I leave this earth knowing only the amounts of money I owe or acquired in a lifetime? Is this a legacy of truth?

When I become aware of my true purpose, mission, and reason for being on this planet, all material gain will come to me in complete, divine sequence. I don't worry.

I make money, time, and friends for myself with the right amount of balance for each.

I make enough money in life to challenge myself, help others, and learn how to grow gracefully through each testing phase.

Everything I do, everywhere I go, and everyone I meet gives me an opportunity for growth materialistically, spiritually, physically, and morally.

☐✓ Checkmark page when learned/memorized

Is the money you are given appreciated, spent, and used for its highest good and the highest good you can think of for yourself?

Money will always help to measure a person's total real worth.

When it comes to making a living, do what you know to be right in your heart, and the money will follow.

When I make money for the right reasons, I will lead a peaceful and fulfilling life.

Work is important and challenging. Finding a reason to live is right. We need to work to live. We do not need to live to work.

Nobody ever wished at the end of his or her life to have spent more time at the office. I spend more time balancing my life. I spend more time on me and those I love in my life.

I learn to polish the skills of my heart. I find a way to work on forgiveness. I dig hard on letting go of ego and pride.

Every day of my life is accounted for. Each precious minute that is spent . . . every second that is used . . . every good thought that is sent to help another kindred soul. I think happy.

If I can keep faith when all is lost, if I can trust internally that I am protected and helped when I have no job, money, or friends—this is my moment of true faith.

To find what I am really looking for, to replace the empty darkness that keeps growing inside of me, I ask internally for help. I ask, "How can I work on my life, for the better?"

❏ ✓ Checkmark page when learned/memorized

When we live our life with balance, giving to others and wanting nothing in return, miracles happen. Things come to us when we least expect them. Wonderful surprises.

It is impossible to heal a wounded heart by making more money. It is necessary to find the hurt and listen to the heart, even if this means taking time off from work.

There will never be enough money in this world to bring us happiness if that is all I am after. Money is a tool to find balance in each and every person's life. It is also the supreme test of the higher self and the lower self.

Chapter 8

RELATIONSHIPS

When we pollute relationships with thoughts that are unloving, we destroy them.

❑ ✓ Checkmark page when learned/memorized

8th Ingredient: Relationships

"My relationships with others complement who I am."

I used to think my life was one hardship after another. Every boyfriend I had, every girlfriend I associated with, every person in my life had big problems and serious issues. I wound up right in the middle of every one. My life seemed to be saturated with depression. I struggled constantly to keep peace with everyone around me. Ironically, the more I tried to help, the more people in my life walked all over me.

What was wrong with me?

When I started sharing all my sadness with different counselors, there were no startling revelations. Then, one day I met with a counselor who was also very spiritual. She told me, "We attract people in our lives according to our karma." As she explained, "Karma is a lot like the Golden Rule. 'Do unto others as you would have them do unto you.' Another way of looking at it would be, you get back from the world what you have put into it.

"Until you lift yourself up to a higher level of thought, you will continue to attract people in your life at the level you are at. Healthy people bore you, Barbara. You seem to want people in your life that you feel the need to fix. You seem to choose unhealthy relationships— with both women and men. You prefer to be in the eye of the storm. Unless there is a daily dilemma, you have trouble dealing with quiet and normalcy." I looked back on my life. Was this really true?

I definitely wanted things to change.

I was tired of being sad all the time. I started working very hard on changing my thinking. I kept my journal nightly. Writing down my thoughts and fears and feelings, I would rate my day. If I gave myself a "1," it was a bad day; if I gave myself a "10," it was a good day. I did this for a month and kept track of my ratings. Not surprisingly, I had mostly 1s. I was not a very happy, fulfilled person. My girlfriends were all battling problems with relationships, alcohol, and divorce. Remember, "like attracts like." The more involved I became with my friends' problems, the less able I was to focus on my own. I looked at my boyfriends in the past. I was always trying to fix things. There were always bad moods to contend with, a feeling that I was responsible for making everything right, the sense that I never did enough.

Why couldn't I have a relationship that made me feel good about myself?

The more I read about codependency, the more I realized that my childhood had had a tremendous effect on my life and the people I brought into my life. I needed to look at counseling and codependency.

I started to realize that if I wanted more love and compassion, I needed to be more loving and compassionate with myself! I was so hard on myself. I had to learn and understand the difference between "caretaking" and "caregiving."

I met again with the counselor who had a spiritual background. She explained to me how we put relationships at risk: we avoid talking about what we are most afraid of. She smiled and said, "Love is not enough in a relationship." I was slowly starting to see the confused signals I'd been given as a child. I now wanted to find a new way. I was tired of dealing with so many problems all the time. My life needed to be filled with laughter and love and lightness.

When we decide to change our life, it can be lonely for a period of time.

Withdrawing from the people in your life who are central, every-day figures is like withdrawing from a drug. I had become addicted to the relationships around me. The phone rang morning, noon, and night. Always there was a new crisis that needed fixing. When I decided to distance myself from those around me who were not healthy, it became very lonely for a while. The phone didn't ring. People got angry. I was given many guilt trips.

Still, I stayed disciplined and removed from my old life.

As I look back, there were perhaps five things helping me the most. The most important was exercise. At first, I went to a health club, sometimes twice a day. I started taking very good care of my body and realized how much my depression was associated with lack of exercise and the food I ate. Second, I fixed my diet. I read Prescription for Nutritional Healing *by James and Phyllis Balch. I also took large doses of vitamins, especially three vitamin B complexes (for stress) and one B_{12}. Third: I took my vitamins at night before I went to bed to help me sleep. I learned to trust in a higher power. God became central in my life and I started to "let go" more easily. Finally, I became interested in me. I did things that made me feel good about myself. I read more books, took a cooking class, bought wonderful tapes to listen to.*

I was determined to fill my day with healthy, happy things to do.

It's easier to write about change than to do it. I know. I have been there.

Each day came and went, and I never looked too far down the road. I know how important it is now to take one day at a time. My relationships with other people are still not perfect. I look at the people in my life and I must say it has gotten better, but some of the drama is still there. We cannot give ourselves a lobotomy about the past. We are the sum total of our experiences, yet we can choose to grow and go forward from them.

People in my life definitely make me feel good about myself now.

> **Key to Ingredient 8: Relationships in my life are healthy, loving and supportive, and fun.**

Reasons for an honest divorce are punitive mental abuse and any kind of physical abuse.

Why does separation take place? Something took the place of unconditional love for each other. I learn daily about loving myself.

When people come together for the wrong reasons, they eventually find a reason why they need to leave. I look at my relationships honestly.

Decisions coming from within the head rather than from in the heart cause people to come together and then part.

Before you stay married for "the children's sake," be sure to ask the children.

There is no officially neutral separation before splitting up unless both parties are deceased.

When there are children involved, people are never completely divorced from each other.

I deal with the breaking up with love and forgiveness in my heart. My head and heart will heal in miraculous time.

"Live" backward spells "E-V-I-L."

When people break up, it happens for a reason, but how in the world do we reason why?

When thoughts become separated from love and we do not trust, we can trust that our relationship will fall apart.

Unloving attitudes, indifference, and refusal to discuss truth ends in two people separating.

If I don't like the effects on my life, if I can't change the negative continuous energy, and if I am sad all the time, sometimes divorce is a turning point from sadness. I am courageous.

There is no person alive who has the right to monopolize, control, and rule another human being. This is taking away that person's power.

Human relationships should only exist to produce love. Otherwise people should meet to regroup and make new plans in the best interest of both parties concerned.

Our species is in trouble because we fight too much and love too little. I start by loving myself.

There is one universal law that overrides all else and can permanently do away with divorce: Love one another unconditionally.

❑ ✔ Checkmark page when learned/memorized

Relationships become polluted with ego, unloving thoughts, and jealousy. Pour ink into a glass of water and watch what happens.

A person who controls another human being only controls the time it takes to destroy the relationship forever.

Sometimes divorce happens when two people have let each other down so hard that neither wants to be the first one to help the other up. Instead they each creep silently away to nurse their own separate wounds.

In a separation, if the intent is to punish the other person, I must be prepared to endure much personal hardship for as long as the hatred and dark feelings persist.

Children are not brought into this world knowing hatred. They learn it from others, but especially in a divorce, from parents.

Once a child learns hatred for a parent, he or she is usually *scared* and *scarred* in some way for life, unless taught forgiveness.

Teach a child to hate a parent when he or she leaves and this teaches the child to hate others, as well as the one who taught them hate.

Leaving a relationship deals with four stages of letting go: denial, anger, forgiveness, and acceptance.

When a person stops believing in someone they stop where they are going in the relationship. The relationship comes to a halt.

❑✔ Checkmark page when learned/memorized

A marriage that does not work is never a failure but rather a lesson to learn from. It takes lots of guts to mature every day. Every hour I am tested and asked to compromise the way I believe.

Separation comes after two people decide that they cannot agree on what is worth fighting for together and choose to fight against each other.

If a relationship is not working, there is absolutely no way that I can avoid change. I can put it off, but it's up to me. New ideas have a tendency to make enemies. They keep popping up at odd times. Maybe it is time I leave.

If a relationship isn't working, and I have intently tried to move forward with forgiveness, and the other party stays in the dark, I may choose to keep the light on and continue to move forward . . . alone, but safe.

Learn to ask for help internally, and know all problems are brought to each of us with the understanding that we will see them as lessons to learn.

We cannot grow only in sunshine. The rain must come to give us healthy balance and understanding of our true identity, which will survive any crisis. Even separation can have merit and purpose. I can grow strong now.

Sometimes in our search through life for our true, higher self, we must discard thoughts, attitudes, and relationships if they are not on the true, spiritual path of enlightenment.

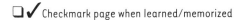 Checkmark page when learned/memorized

Two people can stay together if they pray, grow, care, laugh, and respect each other. Each of us has one day unto herself or himself and together.

Trial and error, avoidance and confrontation, situation and comedy—all constitute the stages of living together with a mate. When we avoid issues, they don't go away. Eventually one of us does instead.

If I lived each day as though it were my last, then perhaps I would have enough courage to talk about real issues each day with my partner.

If our partners are truly mirrors of ourselves and if at one point there must be a marriage before there can be divorce, how can this all add up to the truth about the way we feel toward our partner, let alone ourselves? What is the truth?

Children can survive a divorce if there is an understanding that it is between the parents. Forgiveness is a key factor in showing children the way to live with unconditional love.

We are teachers to, for, and with each other. Each of us comes into another person's life to show the way, open a door, and close a door. Whether or not we make the right choice is up to us.

If divorce is truly the next path to take, there must be no room for the "three thieves" that rob us of our character and time. They are guilt, anger, and unforgiveness.

❑✓ Checkmark page when learned/memorized

Leaving a person must be dealt with in the way choices are explained to children: We tell them they can always choose what they think is right or wrong, but they must be prepared to accept the consequences, go on to the next choice, and *still continue to love themselves.*

There is a reason for everything that I see. There is a reason for you and for me. If I planted a tiny seed and gave it all the sun that it needed but never gave it rain, it wouldn't grow. Like the seed that isn't yet a flower, I should be grateful for this rainy hour, for when I see the sun again, I will know there is a reason.

Leaving someone is always going to be a growing process that can either be delayed or accepted. I can choose to listen to what my higher self is asking me to do next, or I can stay stuck.

We can never achieve happiness at the expense of or without caring about other people. People are in our life for a reason: to learn from them and, if possible, to help them and ourselves.

Two people can stay together in a relationship without a divorce if they are willing to close all the doors that lead to anger, resentment, guilt, and blame.

The death of a relationship is *not* the end of the world. It very often is the beginning of a new and beautiful life. A life that is built on courage, truth, and above all love for one's own self.

Daily I desire to be better. I think more joyously, and I let go of the reasons for anger in my heart toward my mate, especially

□ ✓ Checkmark page when learned/memorized

toward the one person who at one time I had agreed to love forever. . . .

I develop a sense of tolerance for self. I acquire a looseleaf notebook and write each day about sadness, self, and situations. I watch myself grow and learn. When sad, I always learn something new.

Focusing on the other person's faults keeps me stuck. The only way to improve my life after a divorce is to conceive of a better one. Imagine it in your head. I see it. I think it. I believe in a better life for me from this day on.

I open myself up to my anger. I write it down. I describe how I feel. Be honest and tell the whole truth. Find my real self. Nurture this, watch the real me grow. Separation is always a major learning session in life.

Leaving someone brings issues to the front for people and allows them to explain themselves and what is causing them inner discomfort. Once the situation is defined, it is time to begin. Don't go back to sleep. Don't go back to sleep!

When we leave someone, we must realize that we are receiving exactly what we want. The other person is receiving exactly what he or she should be learning from also. This is known as the law of cause and effect—an opportune time to learn so very much.

Separation is a result of withholding love from myself and the other person. All of this discomfort comes from not disclosing the truth. Telling the truth will heal a situation.

❑ ✓ Checkmark page when learned/memorized

The only way in which truth can be seen and used in a relationship is when both parties take full responsibility for all parts of the situation leading up to and including the breakup. They both agree to totally forgive.

I listen to my heart, not my friends, when going through painful situations. Always the inner guidance of love supports and helps me. I ask to be surrounded in light, and I thank God for resolving the entire situation for the highest good of all parties concerned.

When the quiet of the evening surrounds me and I am one with my God and my thoughts, I go behind the circumstances of the situation, and find the love in myself and in others involved in the situation. I try to detach from the emotion.

The first step to healing from a breakup is to learn something new about our belief system. We must take responsibility for our pain. It is okay. We can heal. We create our beliefs. We can go on. We can replace a sad thought. We have power to do this.

Regarding a breakup in a relationship: All improvements in a person's life must begin with "thinking it so." I start with forgiving myself and ask internally to be forgiven. I face myself.

A very important concept to learn in leaving someone is how to move away from selfish desires into selfless desires, and be willing to go forward.

What is more important in life right now? Am I the one who is right, or am I the one who is happy?

❏✓ Checkmark page when learned/memorized

The time comes when we must all face the truth. Blame is not the issue. There are lessons to learn, and we are each other's teachers. Have we learned from this person?

What exactly has this marriage taught me? What did I need to learn, to see, and to grow from? Living through all of the situations that were so painful—what has this taught me about myself?

Can I let go and go on with my life, or do I have to win? Can I let go of the anger and the denial and the hurt and the frustration and say, "I have lifted my awareness of life"?

The perfect partner can only come into my life when I have a "perfect understanding of who I am and what purpose my mission is on earth to fulfill."

❏ ✓ Checkmark page when learned/memorized

Chapter 9

MARRIAGE

*Human relationships exist
to give love.*

❑ ✓ Checkmark page when learned/memorized

9th Ingredient: Marriage

*"I believe a marriage should always be fun.
Laughter is healing."*

I always wanted to be married and feel loved by my husband. Ironically, two people in the same marriage can have a very different definition of love.

In the beginning, marriage started out a lot like going on a holiday. I brought along my hopes for being satisfied and jumped right in, waiting for it to get good. I had no idea how much of my own ego, pride, and personality affected daily married life.

I also did not realize my family background accounted for many of the ways I dealt with things in my own marriage. I had no problem working hard day and night for the material things both my husband and I wanted. It was the emotional issues, which far outweighed the material issues, that damaged our marriage right from the beginning. I kept score and got even.

Married people need to feel needed.

I silently filmed my parents over the years they were married to each other. I used this internal movie as my subconscious barometer in deciding what was okay in my own marriage. Because I came from a very troubled home life, I never saw my father and mother interact on a loving, nurturing level with each other. They did not laugh together or support or nourish each other. There were no hugs, kisses, or affection exchanged. All these things were missing. I thought being cold, indifferent, and aloof was okay.

A husband and wife need to support one another.

I had stored tremendous amounts of anger up inside me, but I did not know where it had gone. I only knew how to act in my marriage by what I saw in my own home growing up. I watched my mother take care of my father from morning till night. In my own marriage, I constantly tried to keep peace even at the risk of compromising my own value system.

Day after day my childhood was filled with a dark dilemma. My mother never had time to think of herself, and besides, after years of the same thing, people fall into ruts. It would have seemed almost ludicrous to imagine my mother wanting to do something for herself, although she had every right in the world to think this way. It had been a common understanding that she was the breadwinner, the caretaker, the scapegoat, the whipping post, and the cleaning lady for so long. Even we children took her for granted in more ways than I care to remember.

If things were going well in my first marriage, it seemed uncomfortable. Could this be "normal"? I felt as though I had to create friction myself. Even if it felt draining, it was far more comfortable to have something to worry about than to have things going well. When my marriage was in a good state, I was uneasy, always needing some new problem myself to solve. After years of therapy, one of the counselors I had been seeing left me with a haunting phrase: "My marriage was only comfortable when there was upheaval."

When things were calm and normal, this was boring for me.

I wish someone had told me that marriage is a partnership between two people who are equal, coming together for mutual inner spiritual and outer physical growth. When I decided to marry, I was twenty-six years old. My first thought of marriage centered on an important fact. "My best friend had just married, so it must be my turn." I put this decision in the back of my mind, and within months I met someone nice. He seemed rather removed, not too interested in dating, yet this was just what I felt I needed. I knew I had met my perfect partner. I was sure this was the person I was meant to marry. I could help change him, make him love me, make him care. He would grow to love me; I was sure of this.

I do believe we are all teachers to one another.

There were many lessons to learn from being married to my husband. I found out quickly how to avoid issues of confrontation. We bought things. We stayed busy and active, morning, noon, and night. I never had a way to measure what was right or wrong in my marriage because there was no one to consult about this in my own family. Things I took for granted as being all right in my marriage were dysfunctional from the start. I had no clue about this. I did not push or insist on any type of counseling, nor did we have any kind of spiritual relationship.

Because I did not look for healing after my first divorce, I jumped headfirst into marriage for a second time. This marriage had more severe problems than the first. Yet, this marriage brought me to my knees. It humbled me to such a degree . . . I finally wanted help. I did not want to live in sadness any longer.

For it is in pain we grow the fastest, one awful day after the next.

If I had my life to start over, I would insist on taking a long series of tests with my soon-to-be husband. I would ask so many questions on love, health, money, sickness, anger, fear, temper, etc. I would take the test I have included in this book and have me and my partner rate each other.

One day a young woman came up to me at a small bookstore where I was holding a seminar. She told me the Relationship Test in my book had changed her life forever. She told me, "Both my fiancé and I took the test. We found, upon finishing the test, that he did not give me a score of ten in any area. Not only that, the part of the test *that required his rating "the most important things to me" were worlds apart from what I felt was most important to me. I couldn't believe how differently we looked at life. It really scared me."*

That simple test opened some very sensitive, raw issues that needed to be brought to the surface. At the end of the day, they parted as friends and decided not to marry each other.

Partners mirror each other.

I quit looking for a partner and started looking for my true purpose.

It became clear that once I was on my own path of awareness, I was not going to continue selling houses forever. There were other new doors beginning to open, one of which was writing. I found myself home alone at night a lot. My writing became my priority, not meeting other people.

I believe that when you least expect it, when you aren't looking to meet someone new, this is when the right person appears in your life.

It was a hot August afternoon. The day before I had just taken my two children to camp for two weeks. I was at an open house for a home I was selling, and was just about to close up. As I went about the house locking doors, I heard a loud roar of an engine and looked out the window. I saw a little green sports car pull up. A tall, good-looking man climbed out of the car. He walked up the driveway and knocked on the door. "Hi," he said, smiling. "I was driving around and got lost, actually I'm looking for a townhouse. S'pose you can help me?"

I wound up selling him a townhouse the following week, and later in the year we were married. I remember thinking back to earlier that day. I had gone to church and said a little silent prayer: "Thank you God for helping me to meet someone new if it is meant to be."

> **Key to Ingredient 9: Marriage takes place for the purpose of learning and growing happily together.**

When a man and a woman decide to live together, they first must make a commitment to each other, promising to respect, love, and nurture each other.

Marriage is admiration of a partner's worth and feeling that admiration, respect, and love unconditionally.

Marriage is one of the greatest tests of human discipline. Each person must live up to the promises that he or she makes to the other.

When you marry, you must try very hard not to use the levels of measurement based on your upbringing. It is important to reach out for a broader value system.

I choose a partner with my heart first, then my head, and lastly, my body. I feel love with my heart.

I create a relationship with someone who solidifies my value system, builds my character, and positively challenges my self-esteem.

I know myself, enjoy life, and find out why I am here before I insist on finding a mate in my life.

❏✔ Checkmark page when learned/memorized

I start each day visualizing my perfect partner. I ask inwardly for direction, help, and higher knowledge. I see my perfect partner coming to me.

Each person presents a puzzle. It is important to learn about a person's family, value system, and spirituality *before* leaping into a marriage agreement.

The only true lasting relationship is built on respect, love, and commitment.

The strongest force in the universe is a triangle encompassing a husband, wife, and higher power.

When two people marry, they both should agree to take a marriage test and grow together spiritually.

Marriage is the only institution that enables people to share, perpetuate, and fulfill each other's wants and needs.

Getting married allows you to test the waters of endurance, patience, and fortitude continuously.

The grass does not become greener once you've been married for a while. If you remove the weeds and remember the fertilizer, how green the grass becomes in your own relationship.

Marriage exonerates an individual from all past mistakes, sadness, and misgivings while it brings with it a whole new set of challenges.

❏ ✓ Checkmark page when learned/memorized

To get and stay married, you have to want, appreciate, and love being married.

Don't think that children will save a marriage. A child is a blessing on its own.

There is no marriage that did not take place for the purpose of learning something.

The only marriage that can survive is one of shared respect, love, and mutual admiration at any cost.

A marriage cannot work with one partner doing all that is expected while the other partner skates by. Somewhere and somehow both will fall down hard.

Being married to a person with whom you are in love allows you to look at the world and its woes with a kind and forgiving heart.

Always marry for respect, love, and laughter, and life will flow along more gently.

If I compromise myself by marrying a person for any other reason than complete, honest, and consuming love, I will regret my decision.

I listen very carefully, quietly, and openly to what my heart tells me about love and marriage.

There may be many loves in my life and ways I have loved, but there is only one true, complete, and fulfilling love in a marriage that lasts a lifetime with two contented people.

❑✓ Checkmark page when learned/memorized

I pay attention to the reason a person is asking me to marry. Am I marrying to find happiness without possessing it first for myself?

Happiness comes from within and the respect and love you feel for yourself must be present before you can be happily married to another person. You must learn to be happy with yourself.

I do not ask of another person in marriage what I would, will, and do not ask of myself.

Dwell not on the shortcomings in a marriage, but rather on what is worthwhile in the marriage.

Marriage must encounter all the peaks and valleys of inspiration, hope, sadness, and loneliness together in order to survive.

Marriage meets every obstacle course with the precision and fine tuning that only comes with daily practice, drive, and determination for growth.

Marriage is a combined agreement. Whatever happens, whoever gets the saddest first will remember how much they love and go easy on the other person.

Marriages are not made in heaven. They can become heavenly with a lot of help, healthy input, and hugs.

Marriage is hard work, but anything worthwhile takes a lot of hard work.

Patience is important with a mate. More often than not, your mate is a mirror of you.

I map out my future with my marriage partner as I would map out my future with a guidance counselor. We are counselors to one another, and our marriage will school us greatly.

In a good marriage, a fair partner monopolizes listening, not talking. A good listener hears the problem every time.

I measure how happy I am in my marriage by how happy I am with myself.

If I allow myself to be a doormat in a marriage, chances are the rug needs to be replaced. I need to look closely at myself.

Marry for money and you may find success. Marry for looks and show off to the rest. Marry for brains and you may pass the test. Marry for love and you've got the best.

Meaningful marriages are not easily attainable unless both parties go into the relationship with their eyes open and their ears attuned to what they should hear, not just what they want to hear.

I can make my marriage happy by working on my own happiness first. I love myself.

Two people who love, respect, and admire each other can live together in a healthy home environment with the benefit of marriage.

❑ ✓ Checkmark page when learned/memorized

Marry a best friend, but make sure he or she is not the only friend.

Find out how happy another person is before jumping into a marriage. What about the person's own family? How does the person feel about a new family?

I make a plan for my marriage before I plan the marriage ceremony. We plan on having a list of mutual goals and values together.

There is not a single way a marriage can be successful without both partners wanting the other person's highest good fulfilled one hundred percent of the time, regardless of personal gain or want.

A wedding ceremony lasts a nighttime. A marriage that lasts takes a lifetime.

Live life with a partner together, yet always hold on to your individual, separate identity.

Marriage can be the most successful, honest, and meaningful way to find true, complete happiness with two human beings.

To enjoy talking, eating, and growing together, with God in the center of the marriage triangle, this is the strongest force in the universe.

Find a best friend in each other and you have a mate who bonds for life.

❏ ✔ Checkmark page when learned/memorized

In our relationship with our mate, we promise to give each other love. The real test exists when we continue to do this through the darkest hour. When it appears that all hope is lost, it is then that miracles occur when one least expects them. We grow strongest in our pain.

It is our hardest and most difficult test when we can look at our partner without judgment and say, I forgive you. I will love you unconditionally whether we live together or apart.

The person that is in our life is there to teach us valuable lessons. If our partner makes us angry and hurts us, sometimes he or she becomes our most important teacher.

Two people come together to bring out the best in each other, have fun with each other, make time for each other, and support each other's position in life. Growing spiritually with each other; this is a marriage.

❏ ✔ Checkmark page when learned/memorized

Chapter 10

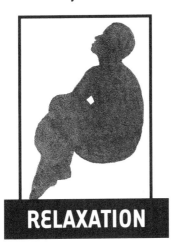

RELAXATION

A few moments of peaceful thought in the morning . . .

❑ ✓ Checkmark page when learned/memorized

10th Ingredient: Relaxation

"I learn to relax in ways that benefit my total person."

As far as knowing how to relax, I still have a long way to go. This might sound funny coming from someone who's writing this book. Yet think about it: how does a person normally relax? My old ideas for relaxing would be to light up a cigarette, make a vodka tonic, and read a good gossip magazine. My definition now for relaxing is "refreshing the body and the mind." I seldom think I ever really refreshed my body and mind, nor did I know how to relax in a healthy way for the better part of my life.

If I became depressed, I rationalized that I needed a drink and all that junk food and chocolate; it would make me feel better.

Drinking was a difficult habit to break. For most of my life, relaxing revolved around having an alcoholic drink. I constantly associated being uptight with relaxing the only way I had seen my parents unwind their entire lives . . . drinking alcohol.

There is not a single person in my life before who ever told me that relaxing could involve quieting the mind, walking out in nature, deep breathing, listening to uplifting music, or visualizing beautiful scenery. Not knowing these other choices made my life so much harder when it came time to deal with stress. I now know how to relax in a totally different manner.

I know one way to completely relax the mind—quiet.

I know relaxing means becoming less tense. The easiest way to do this is by taking a deep breath in through the nose and out through the mouth. I then say to myself, "Whatever is bothering me right now, I can let go of it for right now."

One day a while ago I spoke at a high school on teen depression. Just as I finished my presentation, a pretty young girl with dark hair and glasses came up to me and said that before I started speaking she'd been looking through a copy of my book I'd brought with me. I was so taken aback by what she said to me that I gave her the book on the spot. Her eyes looked so sad, and when she opened her mouth to speak, her sentences began to run together. "I never realized I didn't know how to relax," she said. "I always felt, well, sort of jumpy, and I can't really explain it, but ever since I can remember, my mom has yelled at me all the time. I don't even know what I do to make her yell at me the way she does. I think she is really angry a lot. All my life I have tried to help at home. When I was a little girl, my mother would never do the wash, and we had nothing to wear. Piles and piles of clothes were everywhere. She made me feel guilty for wanting to have clean clothes to put on. My father would go into his den and shut the door. No one was allowed in, night after night. I wish I'd known how to make them happy and relax my body, but I didn't. I was always uptight. Your book taught me how."

More and more often, I run into people who have no clue what I am talking about. Relaxation to them is stopping to buy a six-pack of beer and a pack of cigarettes. How is it possible to change this attitude?

Relaxation comes in a breath—a long, deep breath.

It seemed as if the more I did and the busier I got, the more I could easily rationalize why I didn't need to relax. It became easy to put it off day after day. The added pressure of guilt weighed in as well. There is a tremendous amount of guilt associated with relax-

ing. For most of my life, I did not feel I deserved to relax. I had far too much work to do.

Remember this: Exercise releases those endorphins that are natural stress reducers in the brain. For every half hour of exercise, these endorphins are released. If we did nothing more than deep breathing throughout the day and a half hour of exercise by walking, preferably out in nature, this alone would be very relaxing and remove stress.

Every day now I continue to see myself surrounded in a brilliant white light. I see this light as love. Wherever I am, throughout the day, I visualize this light and it relaxes me. In order to do these things, I must discipline myself to relax. I know this will help me think clearly. The old ways are part of my lower self. The old ideas of taking a drink and lighting up a cigarette are belief systems I acquired from my family. These were not my truths.

Relaxation is with me whenever I want it.

I have found listening to beautiful music to be extremely relaxing. I put on soft, uplifting music during the day and at night before I go to bed. Some nights, settling in with a good book instead of turning on the television is more relaxing. It's difficult to believe so many people actually turn on the television to go to sleep for fear of facing total quiet. "Can't go to sleep any other way," they complain. Well, why not try listening to soothing music or an inspirational tape? I particularly love Celtic Visions, Out of Africa, *and music by George Winston. There are so many other great CDs. Go into any music store and ask for suggestions.*

One of the hardest things for me to learn was to sit quietly in a room without any noise. At first, I tried to do this in small doses, a few minutes at a time. I would just come home from work or from some place especially taxing, and I would sit down in a chair and start to take some deep breaths. It was amazing how quickly I began to yawn. I could feel my body loosen up, and all of me was much more at ease. Little by little, I started looking forward to doing this if even for five or ten minutes. The results were unbelievable. I honestly felt better almost immediately, as soon as I was able to sit down in a chair and just be still for a while.

I know now there are healthy ways to unwind and healthy ways to relax my mind and my body. I feel so much better relaxing with exercise, music, a walk, a good book, a nap, cooking a new recipe, and so many other healthy outlets. I don't miss having drinks and that morning-after hangover. Taking time out of my busy day—a pause to refresh—is essential for relaxing my entire being.

> **Key to Ingredient 10: Every day I must take a few minutes to relax, unwind, and recharge my entire body.**

How can I relax? I take a deep breath, I sit quietly, I focus on my breath, and I breathe in slowly. I do this ten times. I let go of all the rest of my worries for now. I see myself surrounded in a brilliant, pure, white light.

To relax, it is necessary to bring the mind and the spirit and the body together. I let go of all outside influences, concerns, and pressures on my being.

I let go of the trials and tribulations of the day; I find a quiet moment, sit back, take deep breaths. I will begin to relax.

Nothing is so pressing, so important to me, and so consuming that my health and peace of mind take a backseat to the issues of this moment.

Beautiful, peaceful music allows my body to relax and puts my mind at complete peace. I can relax and let go of all my problems.

A beautiful sunset, an early-morning walk, or a contemplative moment of forgiveness are antidotes for peace and relaxation.

I find a "secret place" in my mind and in my heart that I can go to where it's okay. I let all the thoughts, concerns, and moments of my day fade away. I see a beautiful place in my mind, and I can relax.

To unwind and slow down and feel safe, it is necessary to learn that the blankets of the mind keep us buried for as long as we feel the remorse, anger, and resentment.

Reading something inspiring helps me to unwind. I eat food that is good for me to help me feel good. I do something kind for someone, and it helps me be at peace. I take time to go within myself and ask for guidance; this helps me to totally relax.

When I have given the best of myself in a day, judged no other human being, including myself, and laughed at the moment rather than denying it, relaxation will always come easily to me.

How can I be at peace and quiet my mind when everything is falling apart around me? I know that relaxation can only come with discipline. I believe that this day is here to teach lessons. It will pass. I look at how I spend my day, how I play, how much I pray. Can I really feel good about myself and relax?

Deep breathing is a key to relaxation. Breathe in deeply through the nose and out through the mouth twenty times morning, noon, and night.

Exercise releases endorphins, which are natural relaxers and automatic stress reducers. It costs nothing to go for a long walk, hike, or run, or to simply stretch your muscles.

Fresh air brings a fresh approach to every situation. Every day is different both in nature and humankind. Relax outdoors.

Take a few moments of peaceful thought in the morning, exercise in the day, and some quiet moments late in evening. This allows one to have balance and the relaxation one deserves.

To relax the mind, quiet the mind. To quiet the mind, pray for peace. To pray for peace, find a place of solitude. To find a place of solitude, go alone and ask within for guidance.

The body and mind are one. Wherever my thoughts go, my mind will go. I learn to focus on happy thoughts, and relaxation will inevitably follow me wherever I may go.

A brisk walk each day, watching a sunset, just listening to the birds, sitting quietly in a room—these are all positive ways of learning to relax.

❏ ✓ Checkmark page when learned/memorized

There is, in each one of us, a divine self (a higher self) and a human self (a lower self). The test of life is to bring the two together in harmony, peace, and relaxation.

To completely relax is to be able to bring my human self together with my divine self. Here, there is no conflict. There is complete peace and acceptance of life as we know it to be.

Relaxation is quietly reaching the next level within myself in which I believe and know that I am always divinely protected. I need only surround myself in the pure white light. I see white light around me.

Once I relax, I bring the mind, body, and spirit together. I can let go of all outside influences, concerns, and pressures of today. All I have is this one quiet, peaceful moment. *I am safe.*

A secret source of strength is that *I know I must relax each day.* It is imperative each day to my finding my balance. I know that all things work together for my highest and best good.

To be able to take that deep breath (in through the nose and out through the mouth), I close my eyes and count very slowly to a high number. I count until I am yawning. I forget all else. I see myself in light. I feel relaxation setting in. I know I cannot operate under panic. It is important to quiet my mind. I relax my body with deep breaths. My mind is clearing, and I am becoming still and quiet. I am at ease. I am at peace.

❏ ✓ Checkmark page when learned/memorized

Daily, I find ways of becoming relaxed and at peace. I go for a walk; I listen to some soft soothing music. I do anything positive that can take my mind off the problem at hand. I can enjoy this new moment I created.

Every day is a constant struggle to find peace. It never ends. It is a never-ending uphill battle that only ends with our last breath. However, I learn that the power and the knowledge of finding peace is going *within myself* to my "secret place." Here I can be assured that I will, at last, find my own peace.

A very important moment in my life comes to me when I realize that I have the ability to create any moment that I want to—at will. I can decide if I want to be sad or happy or angry or indifferent. I can decide instantly. I always have a choice.

Relaxation comes from removing worry. Worry brings nothing positive. It takes away from creating, keeps good from happening, keeps a wall up in the universe, and stops good from coming our way. As soon as I *stop* my *worrying*, things have a way of clearing up.

The best way for me to relax is to limber up. I can become a little sillier. I take more chances for a change. I try hard *not* to take myself so seriously. I travel just a little lighter. I try not to constantly worry about tomorrow, when today is all that I really have. I can relax completely by creating this moment.

I do three things daily: I try not to worry, I try not to fear, and I try to take care of my body. Today I trust, love, and laugh a lot.

☐ ✓ Checkmark page when learned/memorized

When I let go of worry, and do not fear, there is a feeling of peace that gradually takes over my entire being. I am calm. I accept now.

I can calm my mind if I take this second and say to myself, "This too shall pass, and I am protected from all harm and danger." There is an inner calm that lies quietly at the base of the brain. This is known as my conscience. I have forgiveness in me, and I can now relax.

Listening to my heartbeat, I feel my pulse, I watch my breath. I enjoy a walk and notice this day. I sense the new energy that is within me. I feel the positive flow of light moving in me.

Now relaxation can come if I trust in a higher power. I lie still. I breathe deeply. I close my eyes and focus on a tranquil thought, a beautiful scene, and a peaceful, soothing sound.

It is imperative that I learn to be alone with myself. I can take time away from work, family, friends, music, and play, and I can just relax alone. This is one important way to relax.

In every twenty-four-hour period there is time to relax. I can take a few minutes. Everyone has a few minutes. This allows for a positive change to occur, a time to "recharge my life."

Relaxing with a good friend, reading a positive book, taking a pause in the day, doing deep-breathing exercises, walking around the lake, and listening to a beautiful song are all ways in which one can create peace and relax.

❏ ✓ Checkmark page when learned/memorized

After the day is done, after the work is all completed, after the lights are turned out and I crawl into bed, I relax. *I take a few minutes and thank my God for the lessons of today.*

Realizing how to relax takes no special effort on my part. I can take a deep breath. I can try something new, a positive good book. I can do something I never tried to do before.

If I could start my life over, I would realize that my health is my wealth. Other things fade by comparison. Relaxation helps me to feel good about my entire being.

Listening now, I know what my body tells me. When it is necessary to take time out, I do. When I need to relax, I can. I know I am safe.

Chapter 11

SPIRITUALITY

*Throughout my life I surround myself
in light. Nothing can harm me
if I don't allow it to.*

❑ ✓ Checkmark page when learned/memorized

11th Ingredient: Spirituality

"Our intentions are the only thing God cares about."

For the better part of my life I thought I was religious. I never investigated spirituality, nor did I understand what it meant. When I was little, I went to Sunday school. I got confirmed and have attended church for most all my life. Yet for some reason I always kept my religion and my daily life separate. I seldom questioned my faith or wondered if I was spiritual.

It took a long time to find out that spirituality relates to the soul. This one ingredient solidifies all the others. Understanding spirituality is deciding clearly what I want and making a positive choice to do it. Knowing I can express divine ideas in my mind, my soul, and my body. I feel so much better now, knowing this. It's so true that unhappiness comes from lack of power. So I let go of what I am attached to and let go of my ego and decide to let God in my life.

My spiritual belief in God is what I consider to be "active faith."

The only way I can learn from everything brought into my life is by believing God is in charge and not me. "There are no coincidences." I know I am strong and nothing has been given to me that I cannot handle. God only gives me that which I can handle. I asked to come here on earth, and I asked for my family and all the lessons I have been given to learn from. It took a long time, but now I know fear only robs me of my power. My faith always reinforces my power.

With God as supreme intelligence within me, I start each prayer with a thank-you. I know my prayers are always answered if they are for my highest good and the highest good of those around me. Therefore, I never attach conditions to my prayers. I ask God daily for discernment, discipline, and detachment from my own personality, ego, and lower-self thinking. When I resolve to be so strong as to let nothing upset my peace of mind, I know outside forces cannot penetrate my faith—no matter what.

There's an old saying: "Ask and the door shall be opened." I believe we are given free will to do with as we choose. If you do not want God's help, angelic guidance, or miracles in your life, you will not get them. When we insist on doing things our own way, we bring in dis-ease, congestion, and fear. Our quality of thought penetrates everything at all times around us.

Remember, if we pray during the day, we get spiritual help.

I feel God created my soul and gave me a personality before I came to earth. So my personality is the energy of my soul. When I decide to align myself with positive love energy, I empower myself with personal power, and in comes my spirituality. If I decide I cannot discipline myself, I give myself permission to be irresponsible. The lack of power within me leads me to addictions. So I decide to discipline my life with respect for God.

A man came up to me at a lecture and asked me if the word "Christ" or "holy" was in my book. He told me, "If these words are in your book, I will not buy it, for it goes against my religion." I told him to take the book over to a corner of the room and see if there was anything in my book that went against what he believed to be truth. "Religion is man-made," I told him. "If all religions were removed from the face of the earth and only ten rules were left, we would have a pretty good world. The ten rules being, of course, the Ten Commandments." He left and came back a considerable while later, smiling. He said, "I bought your book." We do not all have the same religion, but we can all be spiritual.

There is one person in particular who has had a significant effect on my life. He was born in a small village. He worked as a carpenter until he was approximately thirty years old. After that, for some time he became a traveling teacher and a preacher. His fame grew, yet he never held office. He never raised a family or bought a house. He never went to college or held any degrees. He was just himself. More than two thousand years have gone by, and still he is considered to be a central figure in human history. Of all the wars that have ever been fought, all the ships that have ever sailed, all the congresses that have ever met, all the kings and queens that have ever reigned . . . no one person has ever affected people on earth as much as he has. This man is my best friend.

Life is easier for me now. Life is happier for me now. Life finally makes sense to me now. I no longer want to row upstream by doing things my own way. I accept there is a bigger plan I am not in control of. I feel I am a spiritual person. I go through life with divine inspiration, angelic guidance, and much prayer. I accept the fact I have this inner help.

I am committed to a spiritual relationship with a God I love and trust.

I have learned to set aside the wants of my lower-self personality in favor of my higher-self spiritual growth. I know now I am here to learn and grow. I also know I have great power when I do not give in to my weaknesses.

There still are times when things get dark. There are times when I doubt and there are times when I cry, but as long as I live and have a breath left inside of me, I know I will continue to be given lessons to learn from. Still, amid any sadness, fear, and loneliness in my life,

I know now I am never alone. I will always have hope. For now I have a recipe to live my life.

Key to Ingredient 11: To accomplish my mission on earth, I must have a relationship with God.

There are at least two purposes for being alive: to help other people and to learn lessons. I feel that learning lessons replaces mistakes.

I am not afraid to go within myself and learn about my true self, my true character, and my true nature. This is who I really am.

There is a purpose and an understanding of higher-self principles infinitely known to all people. One must search very deep and hard to find the core of spirituality beyond religion.

Peace, love, and joy can only be encountered when one truly accepts the "inner truth" that lies at the very core of all.

The present, the past, and forgiveness can be experienced in a breath, by accepting truth doctrine. I am completely letting go of ego, personality, and all fear.

Fear will subside when I accept that there is a greater power that is in control of all the universal decisions to be made. There is nothing to fear except the thought of it.

There is a supreme being, a light within and without that beckons to all of us. My choice lies in deciding to live in darkness or follow the light. Light brings warmth, safety, and security.

☐✓ Checkmark page when learned/memorized

Quiet, solitude, and forgiveness are the "key tools" to learning and accepting spiritual guidance at any and all levels.

I can possess and acquire and achieve all that the earth has to offer in and of a material nature, but when the lights go out at night, the "test of truth" begins.

Beyond religion is spirituality. Beyond spirituality is enlightenment. Beyond enlightenment is goodness, and beyond goodness is the door to all salvation.

There is only one way to live without regret, without anger, and without sadness. That is totally accepting inner truth and all spiritual guidance. It is then possible for peace to come.

How can I find spirituality? I do not need to travel far. I have only to sit quietly, and ask for divine protection and to "live in the light." All the answers I need will start to come to me.

There are no separate heavens for all the religions on earth. There are separate "realities" that each of us brings to the table.

I must be willing to forgive those that have hurt me, and wronged me and mistreated me . . . so many times that I lose count. This is my basis for understanding what "inner peace" truly is.

I treasure all the pain that has been brought to me, along with the good. In my pain lies the path to enlightenment and discernment and true understanding.

☐✔ Checkmark page when learned/memorized

Each day I take a few moments for peace and quiet in the morning, or in the afternoon or the evening. I have quiet, private moments in which to reflect and forgive. The white light of love surrounds me.

It matters not what is in my painful past, for it is gone. It matters not that I fear the future, for it is not here. However, the "precious present" is exactly what I have now to do with whatever I want. I will use my time wisely and productively.

I open my heart to the "closed fist" of anger and resentment within me, and I "let go" of all that is. There, at the bottom of the painful pile of emotional hurts, lies the rainbow of the real me.

I speak gently to myself. I learn about myself, and I go easy on myself. I never will be capable of true, sincere, and honest love until first I can love myself—unconditionally.

I separate all the "just" from the "unjust" and I see that I am given not the "mistakes of life," but rather the "lessons of life." They teach me and help me and enable me to grow inwardly.

Just by reaching out to myself for five minutes and asking quietly and honestly for love and light to guide me to the understanding of why things are, I will see "the light."

Peace cannot be chased or pursued. Peace can only be attained through quiet, reflective, and meditative private moments with myself. This acquires understanding and knowing myself.

❑ ✓ Checkmark page when learned/memorized

I guard my thoughts, and I lift my thoughts, and I choose my thoughts wisely. I know I am then able to aspire and lift my awareness level quickly and effectively.

Powerful Prayer of Protection: The light surrounds me, the light enfolds me, the light protects me, and the light watches over me. Wherever I am, God is and all is well.

Lest we forget: all men are brothers at birth and at death. So why the difficulty in between? It is misjudged reason, separate realities, and ignorance to truth.

The desires of the heart will conflict with the desires of the mind if one is *not* looking at the situation with sincere, honest reason. Always I ask for divine guidance before I attempt to try to solve a situation.

I speak quietly and kindly to others. I will refrain from slandering others. I know there is a universal "law of fulfillment," (what goes around, comes around). The recipe for my greatness does not *contain gossip.*

I will persevere. I will press on. I will keep hope and love close to my heart. I will not look back except to dump, unload, and go forward with forgiveness in my heart.

Freedom from all my fear starts with my willingness to look completely and honestly at myself. I ask inwardly for help. I know that I am watched over, protected, and safe from harm.

☐ ✔ Checkmark page when learned/memorized

One can have sex and be devoid of love. One can have religion and be devoid of spirituality. I have love in myself for me.

When I meditate, I acquire a feeling of timelessness. If I deny this moment and don't take time to pray, I lose sight of God. I know I need to find quiet time daily.

The ultimate truth, beyond diet, exercise, and material fulfillment, is to experience unconditional love, which is the ultimate truth.

The value of a religion that identifies God and the Christ light gives people an understanding of their values in life and the truth within themselves.

When I am in touch with my spirituality, I am able to see the falseness of sickness and disease. The lower self in me fades away and gives way to higher self within me.

If I can stay centered in the light and believe that all good will come from each lesson given to me in life, I will be lifted out of my fear and removed from darkness.

The way to be in the world but not of the world is to proceed along the path of truth. What is the absolute truth each day?

If you can stay centered in the light and believe that all good will come from each lesson given in life, you will be lifted out of fear and removed from all lack and all loss.

The more I can become conscious that my source of all good is in God, the easier my life will become. I know that light is in my life, light is in me, and I see light in all people.

Prayer is a mystery to people. Humanity does not understand the relationship between God and people; however, something within us all seeks to know something much bigger.

The most powerful prayers are prayed with thankfulness first— for example, "Thank you, God, for this situation." I always ask for light and awareness and whether I know it or not, I am praying.

All things are always possible to the one who prays. Faith is an incredible power. Prayer prepares us for bigger things. Prayer is never a matter of words but rather a thought of love.

When I find God, I see my greatest light. This is a light that encircles and protects me from all outside forces. It brings a calm that was unknown to me before.

I am a person who continues to find my higher self within me. I seek God within me and I am not upset by outer conditions. I am able to solve my problems. I know that when I pray, I bring personal power to my life.

I am learning to become spiritual. I am patient. I have trust that I do indeed have purpose in life. I am thankful for exactly where I am at this moment. I am learning lessons from what I have been given to work with and the family that I have been given.

❑ ✔ Checkmark page when learned/memorized

Each morning, noon, and night I ask for divine direction. I say *Thank you, God, for surrounding me in light and love and showing me my true spiritual path that I should be taking. Thank you for dissolving all negative situations in my life for the highest and best good of all concerned.*

When I become conscious of my own identity with my mind as my creative source, whatever I want, imagine, feel, and act enthusiastic about will come to be if it is within divine will and for my highest good and the highest good of all.

All beauty and order are spiritual, within each person. They are inner states of being. Peace can only be found within each person.

To find true spiritual inner peace, I can let go completely of all forms of envy, jealousy, resentment, anger, and hatred.

The art of being kind to one another is all this world needs.

One of the greatest causes of disease in the body is sadness. Because of this, I ask God for help, guidance, and love to come into my life.

No matter how well endowed or well equipped I am, it is not enough for the world to recognize my genius, gifts, or talents. Only the universal spirit can give me new inspiration, hope, and courage to go on.

To complete the picture of my life, I must learn to know myself. Why was I put here? What is my mission and my purpose to

❑ ✓ Checkmark page when learned/memorized

help humanity? Each of us has been given one specific gift and mission to do. What is it?

There are two kinds of emotions: the higher and lower expressions. The lower emotions are destructive and take a toll on physical health. Emotion is power. Constructive emotions give me inner experiences about spirituality without which my life would be dull and ordinary.

To become truly spiritual and renewed, I must let go of all blame. I can now remove all feelings of greed, resentment, anger, and fear. I am safe. I must let go of disgrace, pain, lust, need for approval, pleasure, and praise. When I learn to clear my mind of all this lower-self thinking, spirituality sets in. I become impartial to others and filled with love for others. Calm thinking takes over, and a quiet, peaceful happiness is in everything.

Spiritual practice allows me to let go of attachments to anger, pride, blame, and all the other delusions that come from ignorance of divine truth and high spiritual law.

I have chosen every experience in life to go through myself. Long before I got here, in a soul state, I picked my family, mates, and friendships, even those I have the most difficulty with. I must learn to work out my greatest lessons.

Every day should have a time set aside for daily prayer, meditation, and inspirational reading. These are powerful moments when affirmations are set in.

☐ ✔ Checkmark page when learned/memorized

Our light that goes out from each of us daily helps lift others' awareness by our just "being." Nothing we say or do is as great as just "living in the light."

The highest way of living involves daily praying, having a true spiritual goal, becoming disciplined, looking for the good in others, and seeing the light in every person.

When I am praying, I am talking to God; when I am meditating, I am listening to God; and when I am in silence, I am accepting God's light and love.

A prayer: *Help me to trust your good in spite of my weakness; help me to know that I can continue to pray with an understanding heart; and thank you for showing me how I can help in bringing universal peace to everyone.*

There is a beautiful quiet place. A quiet place that has nothing to do with being still. It lies between the wanting of the heart and the yearning of the soul. Here, the lower human self and the higher divine self are at peace with each other.

Throughout my life, I surround myself in divine light. I know that nothing can harm me if I don't allow it to. This radiant light protects me. I am safe.

God will never give me or any person more than he knows that I or anyone else can handle.

There is no one person that can bring me absolute truth. The real authority lies with God and the truth is within me. I listen to my inner guidance. I know there is an inner teacher within us all. It sees me through any experience I may have.

All major religions are based on learning to rise above human experience and to reach out for spirituality within oneself.

I learn to check my messages internally daily! I drop in and see if my inner self has called for me. I get my inner messages, as I would my messages off my answering machine. I ask for direction, discernment, and detachment—daily.

I spend at least five minutes in the morning and five minutes in the evening with God in silence. I am learning to simplify my life. I am happier.

I am learning to discipline my mind toward a spiritual thought. A disciplined mind accomplishes miracles. I know I can do what I set out to do.

❑✔ Checkmark page when learned/memorized

Today's Awareness

I can now remain centered, calm, and clear,

for no longer do I wage the old battles of doubt.

I am now guided and guarded and gifted with love.

No longer do I feel it necessary to find acceptance in others.

I let go of all my heavy burdens of prejudice, hate, and anger.

No more time for dis-ease, discomfort, and false fears.

I can now believe that I am not alone. I am not alone.

I am never alone.

I see now that I have angelic guidance, heavenly help, and above all God's unconditional love at all times.

I have discovered a recipe for light, love, and laughter in my life.

I let go of the old.

I bring in the new.

I am gifted, grounded, and granted love at all times.

This truly is my higher awareness.

❏ ✓ Checkmark page when learned/memorized

Chapter 12

RULES FOR LIVING

*The highest internal law is
to love one another.*

❑ ✓ Checkmark page when learned/memorized

12th Ingredient: Rules for Living

"Love, forgiveness, and discipline are my most important rules."

Looking back at my childhood, I now know that I didn't really have any upbringing. Because of this, I didn't really have any rules for myself. Even when I went on to be successful in life at my job and making money, I set up my own rules. I secretly prided myself on being so motivated when I really didn't follow any internal laws of discipline.

I knew in order to make money, I needed to work. As I look back again, I realize that those in my family were my best teachers for my career. I realized at an early age that I would be a good salesperson, and I went after this. Yet lessons kept coming left and right, and I did not know I was supposed to learn from them, nor did I know how to learn from them. The people in my life were more of a deterrent than a support system, and I felt isolated. More than anything, I had a big ego, and no one was going to tell me what to do. I had come up the "hard way," I had learned enough lessons, I was on my own, and that's just how I wanted it to stay.

I am aware I am a student of life; I need to learn the rules.

When I honestly wanted to learn about healing my life, I thought I would have to go to counseling for years. I felt my past had so much sadness, fear, and anger in it, I would never be able to heal such pain. It actually took me years of searching for the answers to learn that the door opened to healing the instant I let go of wanting to do everything myself. The instant I let go of all my ego, I understood the rules that were coming to help me.

My body, and all the lessons that have been given to it, is mine for the whole time I am alive. It doesn't really matter if I get upset when I don't learn a lesson, because it will always come back to me again in a different way if I didn't learn it the first time. That's why all situations are important. Even in the failed attempts at getting something right, there is a lesson to learn.

One day I heard a teacher explaining the way boundaries and rules work. She described an experiment in which experimenters removed from a school playground all its fences, leaving the playground open. At the end of the playground field was the street, and traffic whizzed by day after day. The school principal took notes and watched in awe as the children were set "free" to do as they wished.

All of them congregated around a small area and didn't venture into the open field. When the playground fence was put back up, the children ran freely and creatively, coming up with new games that took up the entire playground area. Everyone needs boundaries and rules.

When we have rules in our lives, our lives are in order.

I understand how important it is to have discipline in my life now.

I have learned to discipline my life with love for God and love for myself and my fellow man. I'm not perfect; I don't always love my fellow man, so to speak, and other people still continue to disappoint me and let me down. But I try not to judge people anymore, and I move on if something in my life really bothers me.

My good health depends on my whole being feeling good. This means a calm mind and a connection to spirit. I have learned to investigate and learn more every day about holistic health. The world is filled with temptation, yet with balance in my life, I can persevere and enjoy.

Now I understand that the people I bring into my life are exactly those I want to learn specific lessons from. It is crucial to understand from the rules of life when to move on and how to move forward. More important, now I know a cardinal rule is finding forgiveness. I must learn to forgive others and especially my family for inner hurts and sadness. This rule of forgiveness frees me to do so much more, and I grow tremendously.

As I have learned new rules for living, I understand and accept new relationships that come into my life. I work at that which I enjoy, and I enjoy where I am now. I accept the lessons coming to me. Every day I incorporate a rule for relaxing, and quiet time interrupts my busy schedule.

There are now specific rules in my life that I adhere to.

My day starts with discipline. My biggest temptation is to ignore it. My life is filled with learning. My day is filled with love. My heart is filled with acceptance of the life that has been given to me.

I am who I am—I am a child of God.

> **Key to Ingredient 12: To find peace and life awareness—
> I abide by the rules.**

❏✓ Checkmark page when learned/memorized

Life Awareness Lifetime Rules

1. I COMPLETELY FORGIVE MYSELF for everything I have ever done or didn't do in my entire life.

2. I COMPLETELY LOVE MYSELF unconditionally and try hard to love others unconditionally.

3. I CONTROL MY OWN LIFE. Never turn *my* power over to another person. Never let others control *me*.

4. EVERY DAY I WILL LEARN SOMETHING NEW. Learning brings me awareness and power.

5. I LET MYSELF BE LOVED BY OTHERS. I allow love to come to me. I want to be around people I love.

6. I BRING BALANCE INTO MY LIFE DAILY. I let my thoughts and my body have balanced activity daily.

7. I GO EASY ON MYSELF. Every day I set goals for myself and realize that I succeed in life no matter what.

8. I CREATE MY OWN LIFE. I can ask for help, but in the end, I listen to my inner self.

9. I SEEK TO FIND WORK THAT SATISFIES me and rewards me.

10. I LIVE IN THE PRESENT MOMENT. The past is gone, I live my life in light always.

11. BRINGING NEW EXPERIENCES into my life is something I try to do monthly.

12. I KEEP MOVING FORWARD, regardless of life's challenges. I stay centered.

13. I WILL LIVE BY THE GOLDEN RULE. I know that "what goes around comes around."

❏ ✓ Checkmark page when learned/memorized

14. I CAN CHANGE ONLY MYSELF. I will try not to change any other person.
15. SELF-LEADERSHIP IS MY GOAL. I can blaze my own new path through life.
16. CONTINUALLY I REARRANGE MY THOUGHTS. I let go of old habits and old relationships.
17. I AM A SHARING, CARING PERSON. I only give of myself and expect nothing in return.
18. I STAND STRONG. It is not necessary for me to lean on any person.
19. ALWAYS I CAN SMILE. I can smile at everyone or say something positive.
20. I LIKE TO HAVE FUN. To balance my life, I must be able to laugh and enjoy myself.
21. EVERY HUMAN BEING HAS WORTH. I respect all life.
22. LOVE, LIGHT, AND LAUGHTER control my life.
23. MY HEART DIRECTS the decisions I make in all walks of life.
24. DISCIPLINE DAILY brings "awareness" into my life.

❏✔ Checkmark page when learned/memorized

Daily Schedule for Life

1. I learn to live with my higher self, not my lower self.

Higher Self	*Lower Self*
Love	Fear
Trust	Doubt
Honesty	Anger
Understanding	Mistrust
Discernment	Gossip
Honor	Judging
Discipline	Resentment
Forgiveness	Blame
Humor	Denial
Devotion	Worry
Spirituality	Remorse
Detachment	Lying

2. For fifteen minutes a day I quiet myself either at home or outside. I take several deep breaths in through my nose and out through my mouth. All the while I ask to be surrounded in divine white light and the highest truth possible. I ask thankfully: *Why am I here?* What is my purpose? Why is this situation in my life? Suddenly, a thought, a person, an event, a word may all at once come into my life. A miracle will begin to occur.

3. I say to myself: *Thank you for the highest love and the highest truth that surrounds me and dissolves all negative situations between myself and any situation for the highest good of all concerned.*

❏ ✓ Checkmark page when learned/memorized

4. I also say: I am thankful for this moment and for what this experience is being brought to me to teach me, giving me the courage to know how to learn from it, and allowing me to go on to the next level of enlightenment.

5. I conclude with: I forgive all others for what they have done to me, and I forgive myself for what I have done to others.

6. Throughout the day, I ask to be surrounded in *divine white light.*

7. Silently I say: *Thank you God for surrounding me in love and light and leading me in the right direction that is for the highest good of my higher self while on this earth.*

8. Little by little, I learn to be quiet with myself. I learn to go deep within, and behind the thoughts of the day and the concerns of the night. I quiet the voices in my mind and I listen.

9. First I learn to ask ("ask and you will receive"); then I must learn to listen (and I will hear my true higher self speak to me).

10. I become at peace with myself and others.

11. There is no set way in which spirit will respond to me. Some people say that they see a *white light.* Some people hear beautiful music and angelic voices, and others just experience a warm glow with a deep inner knowing. I am safe.

12. *I need never try hard to find the light. If I but ask, it will find me.*

❏ ✔ Checkmark page when learned/memorized

"*Every day it is important to say positive affirmations. Positive affirmations said daily, throughout the day, retrain the mind to be fearless, positive, healthy . . . and happy!*"

❏ ✓ Checkmark page when learned/memorized

Whenever a sad, angry, dark, or depressed thought comes into my mind, I say affirmations. They work; they help me relax. They help put me to sleep. They help balance me, and they bring me self-confidence.

I am alive, I am alert, I am achiever, I am astounding, I am action, I am amazing, I am affective, I am alignment, I am atonement, I am avenue, I am aware, I am awesome.

I am breath, I am blessed, I am brave, I am beatitudes, I am becoming, I am boundless, I am beautiful, I am best, I am better, I am big.

I am creative, I am courageous, I am calm, I am compassionate, I am clean, I am champion, I am certitude, I am careful, I am companion, *I am committed,* I am changing, I am centered.

I am duty, I am disciple, *I am discernment, I am discipline,* I am dependability, *I am depth,* I am dedication, I am development, *I am decision,* I am devotion, I am detachment, I am diligent.

I am effective, *I am energy,* I am enlightened, *I am evolving,* I am empathetic, I am education, *I am empowerment,* I am electric, I am establishment, I am expression, I am enjoyment, I am exercise.

I am faith, I am freedom, I am fusion, *I am fulfillment,* I am fun, *I am forgiveness,* I am feeling, *I am fearless,* I am friendship, I am family, I am future, I am fountain, I am foresight, I am forever, I am fulfilled.

❏✓ Checkmark page when learned/memorized

I am goodness, I am grateful, I am gratitude, I am gifted, I am gladness, I am genuine, I am generous, I am genius, *I am gentle, I am grace.*

I am health, I am happiness, I am honest, I am humor, I am hope, I am heaven-sent, I am higher self, I am honor, I am home, I am hospitable, I am heart, I am happy, I am helper, I am harmony, I am humble.

I am inspiration, I am involvement, *I am identity,* I am industrious, I am illustration, *I am intuition,* I am impression, I am important, I am imagination, I am invention, I am invincible, I am intimacy, I am improving.

I am jewel, I am just, I am Jesuit, *I am justice, I am joy,* I am Jerusalem, *I am joyful,* I am jurisprudence, I am jubilant, I am jovial.

I am knowledge, I am knowing, *I am kindness,* I am kaleidoscope, I am kite, I am kinetic energy, *I am kingdom,* I am knowledgeable, I am knowing.

I am love, I am light, I am leader, *I am listener,* I am learning, I am language, I am law, I am life force, I am latitude, I am logic, I am location, I am loyalty, I am lyric, I am laughter.

I am movement, I am missionary, I am majestic, *I am marvelous,* I am merriment, I am magnitude, I am magnet, I am management, I am manifestation, *I am meaningful,* I am measure, *I am minister,* I am mother.

❏✓Checkmark page when learned/memorized

I am necessary, I am needed, I am now, I am new, I am nice, I am nature, I am navigator.

I am original, I am ovation, *I am obedient,* I am objective, I am observation, I am occupation, I am open, *I am optimistic,* I am orderly.

I am peace, I am praise, I am plentiful, I am pragmatic, I am poise, I am purpose, I am posterity, I am precision, I am permanent, I am providence, I am passage, I am pathway, I am perfect, I am perpetual, I am pleasure, I am playful, I am position, I am positive, I am possible, I am posture, *I am power,* I am perceptive, I am present, *I am principle,* I am powerful.

I am quiet, I am quest, *I am quality, I am quick, I am qualified,* I am quick-witted.

I am ready, I am relaxed, I am resilient, I am restoration, I am remarkable, I am reflective, I am resounding, I am renovation, I am restitution, *I am radiant,* I am reason, I am rapport, I am reality, I am receptive, I am recognition, I am recreation, I am renowned, I am regeneration, I am reserved, I am response.

I am serenity, I am security, I am stature, I am style, I am stoic, *I am safe,* I am sensible, I am spontaneous, I am sincere, I am satisfaction, I am spirit, *I am spiritual, I am source,* I am secure, I am solid, I am smart, I am special, I am self, I am seeker, I am solution, I am sphere, I am steady, I am strength, I am serenity.

❑ ✔ Checkmark page when learned/memorized

I am truth, I am trust, I am tenacity, I am tenderness, I am temperament, I am thorough, *I am timeless,* I am treasured, *I am transformation,* I am triumph, I am tribute.

I am universal, I am unique, I am united. *I am understanding,* I am undefeated, I am unpretentious.

I am value, I am voice, I am victorious, *I am vision,* I am victory, I am validation, I am vehicle, I am vibration, *I am virtue.*

I am wise, *I am wisdom,* I am whole, I am well, *I am wanted,* I am witty, I am worthy, I am witness, *I am wonderful,* I am worry-free.

I am youth, I am young, I am yearling.

I am zest, I am zeal, I am zip, *I am zenith!*

I try to go through the alphabet and say as many affirmations as I can think of. I say them to myself in the morning, at noon, and at night.

Again, I remember that whenever any negative thoughts come into my head, I can replace them with powerful affirmations. These affirmations give me strength. They remove my doubt and all my fear. I am whole, I am safe, I am protected. I am a child of God.

❏ ✔ Checkmark page when learned/memorized

My Own Rules for Living

I HAVE RECEIVED MY BODY TO LIVE WITH.
Whether I like it or hate it, this body has been given to me to live with for as long as I am alive on earth.

I HAVE BEEN PUT IN THE FAMILY I ASKED FOR.
Whether I like them or not, my family has been given to me to teach me powerful lessons to learn from.

LESSONS WILL BE GIVEN TO ME UNTIL LEARNED.
The lessons given to me will be in all shapes and situations until I learn them. Once this happens, I get more lessons.

DAILY I AM TESTED WITH NEW EXPERIENCES.
I can stay stuck or I can forgive what happens and go forward and grow. Every mistake is a lesson to learn from.

MY SOUL CAME TO EARTH WITH PURPOSE!
It is up to me to find out what my mission is and what talents I have been given to find satisfying work in life.

RELATIONSHIPS WILL COME INTO MY LIFE TO TEACH ME.
The more I let go of my ego and pride, the more I will find a relationship that benefits me and we can grow together.

MY OWN PERSONAL POWER KEEPS ME DISCIPLINED.
When I learn forgiveness on a daily basis I retain my personal power. I forgive and I am strong.

EACH DAY IS GIVEN TO ME TO LEARN AND ENJOY.
It is up to me to discipline my day with exercise, meditation, good food, and prayer.

MY GOOD HEALTH WILL COME WITH BALANCE.
It is my responsibility to eat right, think right, and live right. I choose to live in light daily.

Summary

I hope you have now discovered a new way to deal with your own personal pain. When you ask yourself, "Why did this have to happen to me?" you now have a new awareness to deal with life.

If you are faced with questions like "Why did I have to be born into this family?" you can now see, at a soul level, that you asked for a specific family to learn specific lessons from. Have you learned them? Are you learning them? Can you accept this?

If something has happened in your life that has caused you great pain, and you are quick to relay the incident but slow to forgive because the word "but" continues to surface, go back, look through the book again.

Your own growth depends on how ready you are to forgive all and move forward out of the past. In the great plan for life, it matters little if a divorce was painful or what that person did to you. It matters little if you struggle with a health problem. It matters little if your boss fired you and you lost your job. It matters little if you have one setback after another and you say to me, "I can't handle what keeps happening to me all the time!" Pain helps you grow—one awful day after the other.

What matters most is, what am I learning about myself? Am I becoming a better person because of this? Do I have a health problem that is trying to teach me something? Am I ready to go forward now?

Ask the universe to tell you. Go quietly inside of yourself and ask *Why* is this happening to me? *What* am I suppose to be learning from it? *How* can I grow from it? Every time you do this, you grow stronger and stronger. You become aware of your true self and your real power surfaces.

This recipe book will give you the ingredients to handle any problem, any setback, any fear.

Give yourself a change.

Remember, for added empowerment: Sit quietly, see yourself surrounded by a brilliant white light, and ask, Why is this situation happening to me?

Then, take this book, hold it in your hands, and open it to whatever page you happen to turn to. Look down. See where your eye falls . . . it just might be the right information for that moment.

"Learning lessons will never end.

If I am alive, there is a lesson to be learned.

I trust in my higher self. There is no one else on

this planet like me. Every soul wants to at long

last be found. I want to finally find myself.

I want to stop imitating and envying other people.

I want to say this time, I have found

my path in life at last."

☐ ✔ Checkmark page when learned/memorized